Eating in Paradise
Cooking in Bali and Java

Eating in Paradise
Cooking in Bali and Java

Noni Siauw   Britta Rath

Photographs by Jo Kirchherr

© 2001 DuMont Buchverlag, Köln
Dumont monte UK, London

Translation and typesetting: Rosetta International, London
Cover photograph: Jo Kirchherr
Printing and binding: Appl, Wemding

All rights reserved

Printed in Germany

ISBN 3-7701-7077-6

Contents

Introduction

The traditions of Bali and Java	6
Street food, snack bars and restaurants	11
Festivals in Bali and Java	124
Places of interest in Bali and Java	133

Recipes

Spices and special ingredients	14
Sambals, sauces and relishes	22
Soups	36
Poultry dishes	42
Meat dishes and sate	54
Fish and seafood	68
Vegetable and tofu (bean curd) dishes	84
Rice and noodle dishes	100
Desserts and puddings	118
Drinks	123
Index of recipes	150

The traditions of Bali and Java

Anyone travelling to Java and Bali in Indonesia will discover a land of great traditions which have survived unchanged to the present day. The visitor may well be surprised by the large number of traditions that still mark the life of these islands. To most people, the image Bali encapsulates the whole of Indonesia. The luscious green vegetation, the rice terraces bathed in sunlight and the fantastic play of light and shade appear against a background of the mysterious, haunting sounds of the island. Everyone who has heard the "kecak, kecak, kecak" sound of the dancers of the Kecak or mankey dance with their exotic costumes and seen the incomparable elegance of their movements, everyone who has heard the irresistible rhythm of music by the light of a fire in the evening, or who has admired the delicate movements of the temple dancing girls whose every movement is dictated by the special rules of tradition, will feel as if they have lost all touch with reality.

Bali has been and remains strongly influenced by Hinduism and Indian traditions, and today these are still reflected in the everyday life of its inhabitants. But Bali is also the main tourist region of Indonesia with the popular tourist attractions of Kuta and Legian. In contrast with its idyllic surroundings, Denpasar, the capital of the island, has developed into a thriving city of 300,000 inhabitants, crowded and polluted by exhaust fumes, where modern western life has invaded the island.

Close to Bali is the much larger island of Java. This was once the centre of both the Buddhist and the Hindu spiritual worlds, with Borobudur, the most important Buddhist shrine in the world, and Prambanan, one of the largest Hindu temple complexes. Now however the island of Java is predominantly Muslim.

Java is economically the most powerful island in Indonesia and visitors today

may wonder how Indonesia ever became a dream destination, when its capital Jakarta is such a large, loud, polluted and over-populated city. But by contrast, Yogyakarta is one of the oldest royal cities of Java, which successfully combines its ancient past with new buildings, traffic and the modern way of life, as well as tourism.

Last but not least is the countryside of Bali and Java with its breathtaking landscapes, friendly people, ancient temples, traditional festivals and culinary delights. Exotic plants and animals are set in a landscape of intense colours, with the brilliant, almost unreal green of the rice terraces, the blue of the sea and the black or white sand of the beaches. Rising steeply in the background are towering mountains, which may be bare or covered with tropical forest and jungle, while the fertile slopes of impressive volcanoes are covered with fields. All in all these islands are a true paradise on earth, with exotic fruits and spices springing from the soil. These contribute to the versatility of the culinary traditions of the islands, as well as reflecting their history and various cultural influences.

It was the cloves and nutmegs growing in such profusion on the spice islands of the South Molluccas that attracted Arab and European traders. First the Arabs and Indians arrived in the 13th century, followed by the Portuguese at the beginning of the 16th century and the Dutch in the late 16th century, all of them keen to exploit the richness of the islands. The traders themselves introduced other spices that they brought with them, such as chilli peppers from America, a spice which has become an indispensable ingredient of south-east Asian cuisine. The region also grows cardamom, cinnamon, coriander, pepper, tamarind, garlic, cumin, turmeric and many other spices, contributing to the distinctive flavour of Indonesian cuisine. It also reflects the many cultural influences which have marked the history of the archipelago throughout the centuries.

Already by the 1st century AD merchants and Buddhist monks had introduced Indian traditions into Indonesia, followed 900 years later by Hinduism which is still the main religion in Bali today. Muslim Indian and Arab merchants arrived in

"Anyone travelling to Java and Bali in Indonesia will discover a land of great traditions."

the late 13th century and were followed in the 16th century by Christian traders from Europe. This influx of many cultures and religions throughout the islands' history is reflected today in Indonesia's culture, customs and traditions, as well as in its amazingly varied cuisine.

Unlike the situation in Thailand, the various dishes have not merged to form a national cuisine. Instead, Indonesian cuisine varies among the various sections and social classes of the population as well as according to the region. A major ingredient common to every cuisine whatever its origins is oil or fat, and soya oil is widely used. But certain groups still have their special preferences, which continue to exist today. For instance, the Balinese predominantly use coconut oil and the Javanese coconut or groundnut oil, while some Chinese favour pork fat and others groundnut oil. Dishes inspired by Dutch cuisine will probably use margarine while Indian and Arab cuisine will possibly also use mutton fat.

Many people still use *mynyak yelanthah*, an inexpensive recycled coconut oil. This is oil in which salt fish has been fried, after which the oil is collected and used again. This recycling of oil is motivated by poverty rather than for culinary reasons; in this respect the colourful abundance of the islands of Indonesia gives a false impression, because oil is always expensive and not everybody can afford to use fresh oil. Either way, oil is always used sparingly.

One of the most striking aspects of Indonesia is that today hardly any pigs are bred or consumed there, a situation resulting from the cultural and religious situation of the country, whose main religion is Muslim. But there is one important exception: Bali. Since this island has never been strongly influenced by Islam, pigs are quite common there. *Babi guling*, crispy roasted suckling pig, is a typically Balinese dish, as is *lawar*, a sweetish sausage made from pork and pig's blood. Another Balinese speciality is *bèbèk betutu*, duck wrapped in a banana leaf and cooked on rice grass.

Anyone visiting an Indonesian market will be met by a medley of aromas and fragrances, typical of the Far East. Prominent among these are the many exotic fruits that add to the culinary delights of the islands. These range from the famous or notorious *durian* or stinking fruit – prohibited on public transport in Singapore this fruit may not be taken on because of its offensive smell – to various kinds of mangos, Java plums, prickly rambutans, scaly *salak*, carambola and passionfruit, papaya, pomelo, sawo and jackfruit – the list is endless and varies with the seasons. The countless food vendor carts, food stalls, little snack bars and small restaurants that line the streets further tempt the visitor to sample the culinary delights of these islands. The street Jl Malioboro in Yogyarkarta is famous for its snack bars where the local dish *gudeg* can be enjoyed; it is made from jackfruit with chicken, onions, salam leaves, jati, coconut milk, coriander and cumin. Solo

(Surakarta) is famous for its *nasi liwet* – rice in coconut milk covered with a banana leaf and cooked in a clay pot. Almost every town or region has its own speciality. For instance, *rawon*, a goulash-like dish, is a particularly delicious speciality of Malang in East Java. Madura, a small island off the coast near Surabaya, is also famous for its cuisine, in particular for *soto madura*, a soup, and *bubur*, rice porridge. Many of the small restaurants lining the streets of Jakarta, Java's capital, offer Padang dishes, Minangkabau dishes from the island of Sumatra, or *tongseng*, lamb-based dishes. Visitors to Semarang will immediately detect the influence of Chinese cuisine on local dishes such as *lumpia semarang*, spring rolls with a filling of crushed fish giving them a particular flavour. It is also interesting that the famous "national" dishes of Indonesia, *nasi goreng* and *bami goreng*, fried rice or noodles, also originate from China. They are actually the *ch'ao fan* and *ch'ao mein* which are very popular in southern China. But many other dishes have been influenced by Baba cuisine (Baba or Nyonya is the general name given to the Chinese who live in south-east Asia outside China and who originate mostly from south or south-eastern China). Arab influence is reflected in several dishes such as *sate* or *satay*, small kebabs that are reminiscent of the shish kebabs of the Near East, and *martabak*, pancakes stuffed with minced lamb.

Most Europeans associate the *rijstafel* ("rice table") with Indonesian cuisine although strictly speaking it is not an original Indonesian dish. In fact it was created by the Dutch although "dressed" as traditional Indonesian cuisine. Other introductions by the Dutch include vol-au-vents and little cakes made from sponge cake mixture.

Opposite page: Balinese sucking pig, dried fish, and delicious rambutan.

Women working in the rice fields.

The Balinese are mostly Hindu and known for their elegant temple offerings presented on religious festivals. Java on the other hand is predominantly Muslim.

A traditional Indonesian meal is not divided into courses, nor are there any set meal times. People eat whenever they are hungry and Indonesians start cooking at dawn. In fact, as soon as the sun begins to rise the streets fill with the sweetish aroma of steamed sticky rice and pandanus leaves emanating from stalls and from houses where housewives are busy preparing food for the family. Traditionally, Indonesians eat throughout the day. The food is available as if from a buffet which is replenished whenever necessary. The dishes should always include fish, meat, poultry and vegetables. But it is perhaps even more important that the preparation should be varied. An Indonesian cookery book could indeed be divided according to the type of preparation: frying, wrapped, roasted, dried, stewed, grilled, steamed, baked, watery and thin, sauté, fresh and preserved. The aroma and presentation of the food is also very important. A well-composed selection of dishes should combine all these aspects – and if the host is a Baba, ying and yang should be in perfect harmony as dictated by ancient Chinese culinary and medicinal traditions.

Last but not least, there is the religious aspect. In Indonesia food is also considered a religious offering, ranging from small rice offerings – *sesajen* – to lavish "tree offerings" – *gebogan* – or entire dishes that are consumed by the family after the ceremony.

Street food, snack bars and restaurants

Indonesia is a country where food is cooked everywhere and at any time, where food is carried through the streets on poles or on carts, and where food stalls and pleasant restaurants line the streets, tempting passers-by with mouthwatering dishes. There are typical dishes for every time of the day and housewives often may not cook themselves, relying instead on street vendors with carts (known as *kaki lima*), rushing out when they hear the distinctive hammering, ringing or knocking sounds with which they announce their arrival and identify the kind of food they sell. The food prepared by the *kaki lima* vendors often complements various home-made dishes.

There are several kinds of snack bars and restaurants in Indonesia. But the country is particularly famous for its typical food stall restaurantsk known as *warungs*, built as simple bamboo huts or today often a tent-like construction. These simple constructions ususally have a few wooden or melamine tables, a couple of benches and a cooking area. Often people just sit on the ground, although this is not often the case in towns. The food is served is frequently served on banana leaves instead of on plates, and the fingers of the right hand are used

12 | EATING IN PARADISE

The range of food and dishes offered by Indonesian food stalls and street vendors is very wide. Arabian-inspired pancakes, *martabak*, *ketupat*, *satay*, grilled fish and fruit – each snack bar and stall has its own speciality.

> "Indonesia is famous for the great variety of its cuisine".

instead of a knife, fork and spoon. These food stalls will offer a variety of dishes depending on the region, the owner's place of origin and perhaps too according to the fashion of the day. In Jakarta, for instance, there are Jawa Timur *warungs* serving East Javanese dishes, and Warung Tegal stalls, or *wartegs*, named after the town in central Java that is a centre of *becak* cyclists (bicycle rickshaws). This is a reminder of the origins of the Indonesian food stall: a place where the bicycle rickshaw could rest and eat inexpensive, home-made food for lunch.

As mentioned earlier, even food stalls are influenced by fashion. For instance, there are very popular places secializing in serving freshly caught, grilled fish, while others serve *ayam goreng*, roast chicken. Inevitably, such widespread culinary trends may cause some regional dishes to fall into oblivion, and in some cases this has probably already happened. Foreign fast-food chains, particularly American ones, have also appeared on the market.

In this connection, disparaging remarks are often made about the "Europeanization" of Indonesian cuisine. But this development should not be condemned entirely. Naturally, it is a bad thing if "Europeanization" should mean that all Indonesian cuisine is changed to suit the palate of Western visitors, thus leading to "standard dishes". However, the changes observed both in Indonesian restaurants in Europe and in Indonesia itself are often the result of a greater variety of ingredients being available and an improvement in quality. They also reflect economic and cultural changes. Indeed, why should a chef not be allowed to improve on a traditional recipe? Why should Indonesian cuisine and Indonesian chefs not be allowed to be creative in their cooking? It would hard to imagine French cuisine today without admitting the influence of nouvelle cuisine.

But back to Indonesian *warungs*. Locals know exactly which cook or which food stall prepares a particular dish best. A person may become famous and acquire a particular standing through excellent cooking, and a speciality may even become a fashionable dish. One woman in central Java became famous for her

delicious chicken cooked in coconut milk and spices, then fried and served with *sambal bajak*. People flocked from all over the area to eat it on the premises or take it away with them. As a result, numerous food stalls sprung up all over the country offering *Ayam goteng Mbok Berek*, or Roast chicken à la Madame Berek. In a way this was an unfortunate consequence because when a dish is replicated on such a large scale, it loses its soul and just becomes a blatant moneyspinner.

Whether from a rich or poor household, few Indonesians will ignore the delicacies of the *kaki lima* or *warung*. But not everyone will go to the food cart or stall in person; they may be forbidden to do so by the family's position or religious views. For instance, people influenced by Dutch traditions will are unlilkely to visit a simple restaurant, preferring large, pleasant but expensive restaurants such as the Oasis in Jakarta, renowned for its *rijstafel*.

Spices and special ingredients

Note: Many of these specialist ingredients are available in oriental shops and supermarkets. It is best to use the original ingredients where possible, but in many cases acceptable substitutes have been suggested.

Abon: Dry, baked or fried spiced fibrous meat prepared from beef.
Asparagus beans: See *kacang panjang*.
Aubergines (eggplants): In common with many of the cuisines of Asia, Indonesian cooking also uses small white, greenish-white and yellow aubergines as well as the larger purple aubergines that are common in Europe and America. *Terong ijo* (small, round, greenish-white aubergines) can also be eaten raw, unlike the purple variety, which must be cooked.

Banana leaves: These serve a number of functional purposes in Indonesian cuisine. They are used as plates and as a lid when braising or cooking. Many dishes are cooked in banana leaves which convey their mild, sweetish aroma to the food.

Bananas and **banana flowers**: There are many kinds of bananas in Indonesia, usually more aromatic and sweeter than those that are commonly sold in the western world. Some are known as cooking bananas. Banana flowers are used to add an elegant, delicate touch to many dishes. These can sometimes be found in florists.

Basil: Three different kinds of basil are widely used in Indonesian cuisine. Lemon basil is particularly popular because of its pleasant lemon aroma. If it is not available, it can be replaced by a mixture of ordinary sweet basil and lemon balm. Dark red basil, known as holy basil, has a sharper taste. Last but not least is Thai basil, which has a taste not unlike aniseed.

Bean paste: See *taosi and taoco*.

Belimbing wuluh: This relative of the carambola or star fruit is widely used in Indonesia. Like the star fruit it is green to yellow-green and has a rather sour taste.

Cardamom: This is available as a seed pod (brown or green) or as already ground seeds.

Chilli and **rawit (cabe rawit)**: Chilli and rawit play an important part in Indonesian cuisine. Westerners should use them with care because of their relatively sensitive palate and stomach. The red and green chillies used in Indonesian cooking are about 10 cm/4 in long and as thick as a thumb. Rawit or cabe rawit are considerably hotter.

Chinese chives: Although of a different species, these are similar to the chives grown in Europe and America but they have sturdier stems and a light garlicky taste.

Coconut cream, coconut milk (santan): These are both are made from the flesh of fresh coconut. The cream has a paste-like consistency and is made from the coconut flesh without the addition of liquid from the coconut. The milk consists of grated coconut flesh to which coconut water is added. This mixture is squeezed and the resulting liquid is strained through a sieve, the process being repeated several times. Cans of coconut cream and coconut milk are sold in oriental food shops.

Coconut water: This is the sweetish, almost clear liquid in the hollow centre of the coconut.

Coriander: Coriander leaves (cilantro) are an important ingredient in many oriental dishes, including Indonesian ones. Coriander seeds, either whole or ground, are used in many kinds of mixed spices.

Cumin: Usually ground before being added to the food, cumin has a bittersweet aroma.

Dèndèng: Very thin slices – almost shavings – of beef, flavoured with spices and sun-dried. They are served fried with rice-based dishes.

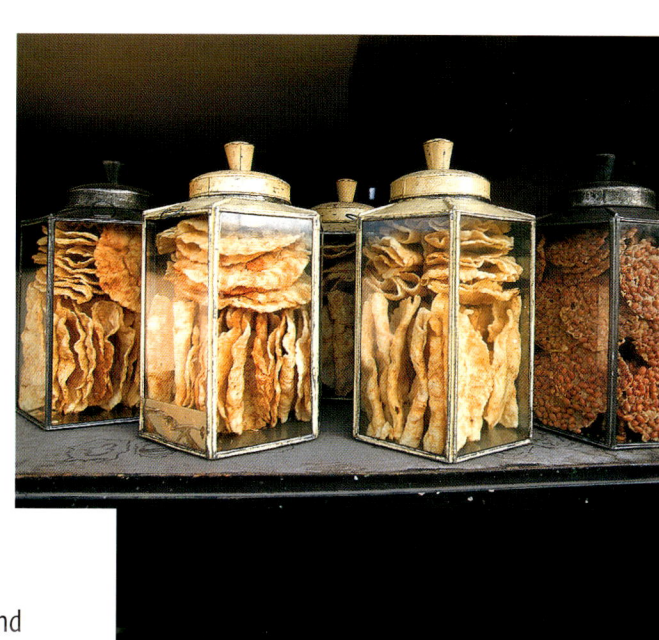

Emping melinjo.

Flowering cabbage (sawi kembang).

Emping: Crisp, wafer-thin pancakes made from the seeds of the gnetum tree. Fried or simply dried, they are available in oriental food shops.

Five-spice-powder: This Chinese spice mixture includes star anise, Szechwan pepper, cinnamon, fennel seeds and cloves, all finely ground together.

Flowering cabbage: See *sawi kembang*.

Galangal root: Related to ginger and similar in appearance, galangal root stimulates the appetite. It is slightly reddish in colour with a light peppery taste. It can be bought fresh or as powder. Also known as *laos*.

Ginger: Fresh ginger is used in many Indonesian recipes. It should be peeled and chopped before cooking or frying.

Hoisin sauce: Another sauce that is made from soya beans. It also includes garlic, sugar and other spices giving it its very distinctive taste.

Ikan teri: Also known as *teri*, *ikan teri* are anchovies. They are usually dried in order to preserve them, since like all fresh fish, they go off quickly.

Jati leaves: The leaves of a kind of Indonesian oak tree.

Jawa pepper: This is a kind of black pepper, slightly sweeter and milder than the normal black pepper, with which it may be replaced if necessary.

Kacang panjang (asparagus beans): These green beans can grow up to 50 cm/20 in long. Their taste is quite similar to French (string) beans.

Kaffir lime leaves: These are used in many Indonesian dishes to add a distinctive flavour of limes, particularly in recipes based on seafood.

Kangkung or **water spinach**: This owes its name to the fact that it grows in or on ponds. The leaves are smaller and more tender than those of the spinach of the west. If it is not available, it can be replaced by watercress or normal leaf spinach.

Kecap asin and **kecap manis**: Indonesian cuisine uses two kinds of soy sauces. *Kecap asin* is a savoury soy sauce, while *kecap manis* is sweet soy sauce the darker and thicker.

Kecap ikan: A salty fish soy sauce.

Keluwek: *Keluwek* comes from the seeds of the pangi tree, which grows in Java and Bali. Warning: this ingredient can be poisonous if it is not prepared properly. Clean the skin carefully with a brush and leave to soak for at least 24 hours. Also, watch out for the smell. Any foul-smelling seeds should be discarded immediately.

Kemiri nuts: These nuts from the candlenut tree are crushed or grated and

Saffron

Kaffir limes

used to flavour sauces. Warning: these nuts must not be eaten raw because the oil they contain is poisonous when uncooked. They can be frozen to prevent them becoming rancid while always being available. If necessary, they can be replaced by macadamia nuts, which are very similar.

Kencur: Spice with an aroma resembling that of ginger.

Kerupuk or **prawn crackers**: There are many kinds of *kerupuk*. In Cirebon, a port on the northern coast of Java, ground shrimps are added, while elsewhere fish may be used instead of shrimps. But there are also simple types of *kerupuk* without any such fancy additions. It is bought dried and deep-fried in hot oil.

Kerupuk rambak, kerupuk kulit: Crisp beef skin. This is sold dried but uncooked. It is wafer-thin beef skin with a little fat that has been salted and dried. It is deep-fried like ordinary *kerupuk* or prawn crackers.

Kunci: Like *galangal*, turmeric, ginger and *kencur*, kinci is a root plant. It has a mint-like taste.

Lalaplan: This term refers to blanched vegetables or raw ones that are dipped in a *sambal* and eaten.

Lemon grass: Fresh lemon grass or *sereh* is used in many dishes, especially fish and seafood, because of its very distinctive aroma and flavour. Usually only the white, woody part of the stem should be used. As with leeks and spring onions, the outer leaves should be removed. It freezes very well.

Macadamia nut: These can be used as a replacement for *kemiri* nuts.

Manisah: A small, firm fruit and member of the gourd family. It resembles kohlrabi, which may be used instead if *manisah* is not available.

Oil: Indonesian cuisine uses several kinds of oil including soya bean oil, coconut oil and groundnut oil.

Oyster sauce: Made from soy sauce and oysters, this has a sweetish-salty taste.

Pak choi (also **bok choy**): This vegetable is very similar to Swiss chard in appearance, but with much smaller mid-green leaves, with whitish stems. It has a mild, mustard-like taste. If not available, Swiss chard or fresh spinach leaves may be used to replace it.

Palm sugar: This sugar is obtained from the sap of the coconut palm. Palm sugar is sold as a very thick paste in a glass jar or in brown coin-like discs about 45 mm/1¾ in across and 7 mm/¼ in thick. If it is not available, brown sugar can be used instead.

Pandanus leaves: These leaves of the screwpine tree add a sweet, vanilla-like aroma to food.

Petéh: Made from the kernels of the large, green vegetable-like pods, sometimes known as stinkbeans, of trees that look as if they are producing vegetables.

Petis: Black crab paste, a speciality of East Java.

Rawit: See chilli.

Rice straw mushrooms: These brown mushrooms are grown on rice straw, hence their name. They are sold in cans in well-stocked delicatessens and oriental food shops. They are very popular in Indonesian, Chinese and other cuisines of the Far East. If not available, ordinary mushrooms can be used instead.

Rice vinegar: Three kinds are widely used in Indonesian cuisine. As well as the normal colourless rice vinegar, there are also black rice vinegar and red rice vinegar. Black rice vinegar is made from black sticky rice and has an aroma very similar to balsamic vinegar. Red rice vinegar, made from red rice, has a sweetish taste and is often used to accompany steamed fish.

Rice wine: Indonesian cuisine uses mostly Chinese rice wine, the most famous of which is that from the Shaoxing region. If it is not available, Japanese rice wine or dry sherry may be used instead.

Rocket: Pungent leaf with a mustard-like taste. If it is not available, it can be replaced with another green leaf vegetable such as Swiss chard, which is however milder in taste.

Saffron: One of the most expensive spices in the world, the orange-coloured filaments of the saffron crocus are now sold everywhere, packaged in very small amounts.

Salam leaves: These are the leaves of a member of the *Lauraceae* or bay laurel family. The leaves are slightly broader and their aroma more intense than those of the bay tree grown in the west, but these bay leaves can be used as a substitute if necessary.

Sawi kembang or **choi sam (tjaysiem):** This "flowering cabbage" has yellow flowers.

Sayur asin: Pickled vegetables, namely rocket preserve, which can be bought ready-prepared in oriental food shops.

Sesame oil: This oil is not normally used for frying but added to dishes in very small amounts as a seasoning during the cooking process. It is obtained from roasted white sesame seeds.

Sesame seeds: These white seeds are often added as a garnish. They are also used in many dishes for their intense nutty flavour.

Shallots (bawang merah or **berambang):** White and red shallots, cultivated like garlic and also widely used in European cuisine. The Indonesian *bawang merah* (red shallots) are smaller than the traditional western shallots, so if the latter are used instead the amounts should be halved. They should be reduced even more if using onions.

Shiitake mushrooms: These are available fresh and dried in oriental food shops, well-stocked delicatessens and some supermarkets. Dried shiitake mushrooms have a particularly intense taste.

Shrimp paste: See *trasi*.

Soya bean sprouts: These are larger than mung bean sprouts, which may be used instead if necessary.

Soy sauce: See *kecap*.

Tamarinds

"Exotic fruit and spices which quickly attracted the attention of Arab and European merchants also contribute to the delights of Indonesian cuisine."

Star anise: This spice is the seed of a kind of magnolia and its name is appropriate; the seed pods each contain a brown seed looking like a small brown star. The taste is reminiscent of liquorice.

Star fruit: See *belimbing wuluh*.

Tamarind mousse, tamarind water: The mousse is made from the brown, pod-shaped fruit of the tamarind tree or *asam*. It has a sweetish, sour taste. If not available, tomato puree can be used instead. Available in oriental food shops, tamarind is normally sold in the form of blocks or in jars. Tamarind water is made by soaking a piece of tamarind in hot water, squeezing it out and using the liquid.

Taoco and **taosi**: *Taoco*, yellow bean paste, and *taosi*, black bean paste, are both used in Indonesian cooking. They are made from fermented yellow or black soya beans. Bean paste is available in oriental food shops.

Tempe: Like tofu, tempe is made from soya beans. It is usually manufactured by small family businesses. The traditional, non-industrial method of production is as follows. The soya beans are cooked until half-done and left overnight. They are then shelled by hand and cooked until done.

The water is poured away and the beans are placed in a container, often a large, flat bamboo basket, in which they are left to cool. After this the beans are placed in water containing yeast to allow the fermentation process to start. The beans are then placed in rectangular moulds, covered and weighted down. They are left to ferment for two days after which the tempe is ready.

Teri: See *ikan teri*.

Terong: See aubergines

Tofu (bean curd): Tofu is made from soya beans (soybeans) and is one of the most widely used ingredients of oriental cuisine, readily available in many supermarkets, health food shops and oriental food shops. It has little taste of its own but easily absorbs the flavours of other ingredients. Because of its high protein content it is a healthy substitute for meat, so it now also plays a major part in vegetarian cooking. In many oriental dishes, however, it is used in combination with meat or fish. Tofu is stored in water (which should be changed every day) in the refrigerator where it will keep for a few days. This is in fact the traditional way of keeping tofu. Tofu is made by soaking the beans, boiling them and making them into a puree; this mixture is then made to coagulate by the addition of vinegar and strained to remove all liquid. It is stored in water in refrigerated conditions until it is sold.

Trasi: This is shrimp paste, a very popular seasoning which is used in many dishes in Java and other Asian countries. The paste can be bought in oriental food shops and keeps for a long time in a sealed container in a refrigerator. Traditionally, it is made as follows. Small shrimps are laid out to dry in the sun, then mixed with salt and laid out in the sun again to dry further. It is then ground into a paste and placed for a week or two in a sealed container. The paste is then laid out once more to dry and then ground into a paste again. This process is repeated several times. Finally, the paste is pressed into a square or round shape, dried again (which prevents it from going bad) and packed. *Trasi* adds a very distinctive taste to food which is always detectable.

Turmeric: Related to ginger, this brilliant yellow ground powder spice stimulates the digestion.

Sambals, sauces and relishes

Sambal is basically a very hot paste made from chilli peppers. The art of Indonesian cuisine lies in the combination of the right sambal or sauce with the correct dish. This is why sambals have such a prominent place in this book. A sambal may be a dish in itself, or it may complement another dish as a condiment, or it may be an ingredient in a recipe.

Sambal ulek

This classic version is also used as a base for many sauces, so it is a good idea to prepare a large amount in advance. It will keep in the refrigerator for a long time without difficulty. If it looks a little dry as a result of being stored for a while, simply add a little water and stir it in.

Method
Remove the stalks of the chillies if necessary and wash. Put in a mortar with salt and sugar and crush to a paste, or puree in the blender.

500 g (18 oz) red chillies
200 g (7 oz) red rawit (small red chillies)
about 1 teaspoon salt
pinch of sugar

Sambal kecap

Method
Finely chop the rawit, cut the shallots into thin slices, and peel and chop the garlic. Add the soy sauce and salt and stir. Finally add the lemon juice and stir again.

5–10 red rawit
3 small shallots
2 cloves garlic
juice of half a lemon
5 teaspoons kecap manis (sweet soy sauce)
pinch of salt

Sambal bajak

One of the basic ingredients of Nasi goreng is actually a variation on this sambal.

Method
Peel the shallots and stir in all the other ingredients, except for the palm oil. Crush together in the mortar, then fry in the oil.

5 shallots
5 red chillies
10 red rawit
2 teaspoons trasi (shrimp paste)
about 1 teaspoon tamarind
2 tablespoons palm sugar
2 tablespoons palm oil

Sambal is also served with vegetable dishes, for instance with Terong bajak (Fiery aubergines: recipe page 90), which is prepared with Sambal bajak. The bamboo tubes next to the aubergines are used for storing sugar.

Sambal goreng

7 shallots
3 cloves garlic
2 red chillies
2 green chillies
1 piece galangal root,
  about 2 cm/¾ in long
½–1 teaspoon trasi (shrimp paste)
2 salam leaves (or bay leaves)
3 kaffir lime leaves
2 teaspoons tamarind water

A basic sauce but not a true sambal.

Preparation
Peel the shallots and cut into thin slices, peel the garlic and chop finely. Remove the stalks of the red and green chillies, wash and cut diagonally into about ½ cm/⅜ in wide strips. Peel the galangal roots and mash. Reserve a few slices of the shallots to use as a garnish. Fry the remaining shallots in oil with the garlic, trasi and chillies. Add the salam leaves, kaffir lime leaves and tamarind water and simmer briefly. If tamarind water is not available, use 1 teaspoon lemon juice and 1 teaspoon tomato puree instead.

Sambal taoco

100 g/3½ oz red chillies
1 tablespoon taoco (yellow bean paste)
pinch of salt, pinch of sugar

Preparation
Crush all the ingredients together in a mortar.

Sambal teri

Preparation
Crush the red chillies in a mortar. Remove the basil leaves from the stalks. Peel and slice the onions. Fry the onions with peeled and crushed garlic, trasi, teri and brown sugar in a little oil. Season with salt and lemon juice.

100 g/3½ oz red chillies
1 sprig lemon basil (or lemon balm and basil)
100 g/3½ oz red onions
3 cloves garlic
1 teaspoon trasi (shrimp paste)
1 handful teri (anchovies)
1 tablespoon brown sugar
juice of 1 lemon
pinch of salt

Sambal terong

Preparation
Crush the chillies, add sugar, salt and rice vinegar (to taste) and stir well. Wash the aubergines (eggplants) and cut into very thin slices. Add to the chilli paste and stir.

Warning: Ordinary purple aubergines must not be used for this dish. They are poisonous in their raw state. Do not try to make this sambal if the small greenish-white oriental aubergines are not available. They are often found in oriental food shops and sometimes in well-stocked delicatessens.

1 handful green chillies
pinch of sugar
pinch of salt
rice vinegar
5–7 terong ijo (small greenish-white oriental aubergines)

Sambal kecap brambang bawang

Preparation
Chop the chillies into small pieces, peel the garlic and cut into thin slices, peel the onions and cut into thin rings. Add the sweet soya sauce and lime juice and stir. Season with salt.

1 handful small green chillies
3 cloves garlic
3–4 red onions
1 tablespoon kecap manis (sweet soy sauce)
juice of 1 lime
pinch of salt

Pineapple sambal

3 slices pineapple (preferably fresh,
    otherwise canned)
about 10 red and green chillies
rice vinegar
pinch of salt

This sambal is delicious served with grilled fish, prawns orto lobster.

Preparation
Cut the pineapple slices in small pieces and puree. Cut the chillies into small rings. Add the chillies to the pineapple puree and stir well. Season to taste with salt and rice vinegar.

Sambal petis

1 tablespoon petis (black crab paste)
2 tablespoons Sambal trasi (recipe
    page 29)
juice of 1 kaffir lime (or normal
    lemon)

This sambal is served as a dip with fruit, for instance mango or sour apples. It is also good with blanched vegetables such as cabbage.

Preparation
Mix all the ingredients together and stir well.

Sayur asin sambal

100 g/3½ oz sayur asin (pickled
    vegetables, such as piccalilli)
3 tablespoons Sambal petis (recipe
    above)

This sambal is served as an accompaniment to steamed rice and also with fried chicken or fish.

Preparation
Cut the pickled vegetables into small pieces, add to the Sambal petis and stir well.

Tomato sambal

- 2 cloves garlic
- 2 tomatoes
- 2–3 red onions
- 3 kaffir lime leaves
- 3 tablespoons Sambal trasi (recipe page 29)

Instead of being served cold, this sambal may also be cooked in groundnut or palm oil. If pieces of meat, fish or crab are added it makes a complete dish.

Preparation
Peel the garlic and chop finely. Cut the tomatoes into fairly small cubes. Peel the onions and cut into thin slices. Cut the kaffir lime leaves into wafer-thin strips. Add the sambal trasi and stir well.

Sambal manis

Sweet sambal

Mix 3 tablespoons Sambal ulek (recipe page 23) with 1 tablespoon brown sugar.

Sambal trasi

Indonesians often eat Sambal trasi with dried salt fish, and in fishing villages this is a traditional poor man's dish. It is delicious served with fried tofu or tempe.

Preparation
Peel the cloves of garlic and puree all the ingredients.

200 g/7 oz red and green chillies
1 teaspoon salt
3 cloves garlic
1 tablespoon trasi (shrimp paste)
juice of 1 lemon or lime

Sambal kemangi

Preparation
Remove the lemon basil leaves from the stalks and wash carefully. Add to the lemon juice and Sambal ulek and stir well. Like Tomato sambal, Sambal kemangi can also be fried. It is delicious served with *lalapan*, blanched vegetables.

1 sprig white lemon basil (or lemon balm and basil)
2 tablespoons Sambal ulek (recipe page 23)
juice of 1 lime

Sambal jeruk

Preparation
Peel the lime and cut into thin slices. Add to the Sambal ulek and stir well. It is an excellent accompaniment to steamed fish.

3 tablespoons Sambal ulek (recipe page 23)
1 lime

Sambal cuka

Sambal cuka is very similar to Sambal jeruk but rice vinegar is used instead of the lime. This sambal is also very good served with steamed dishes.

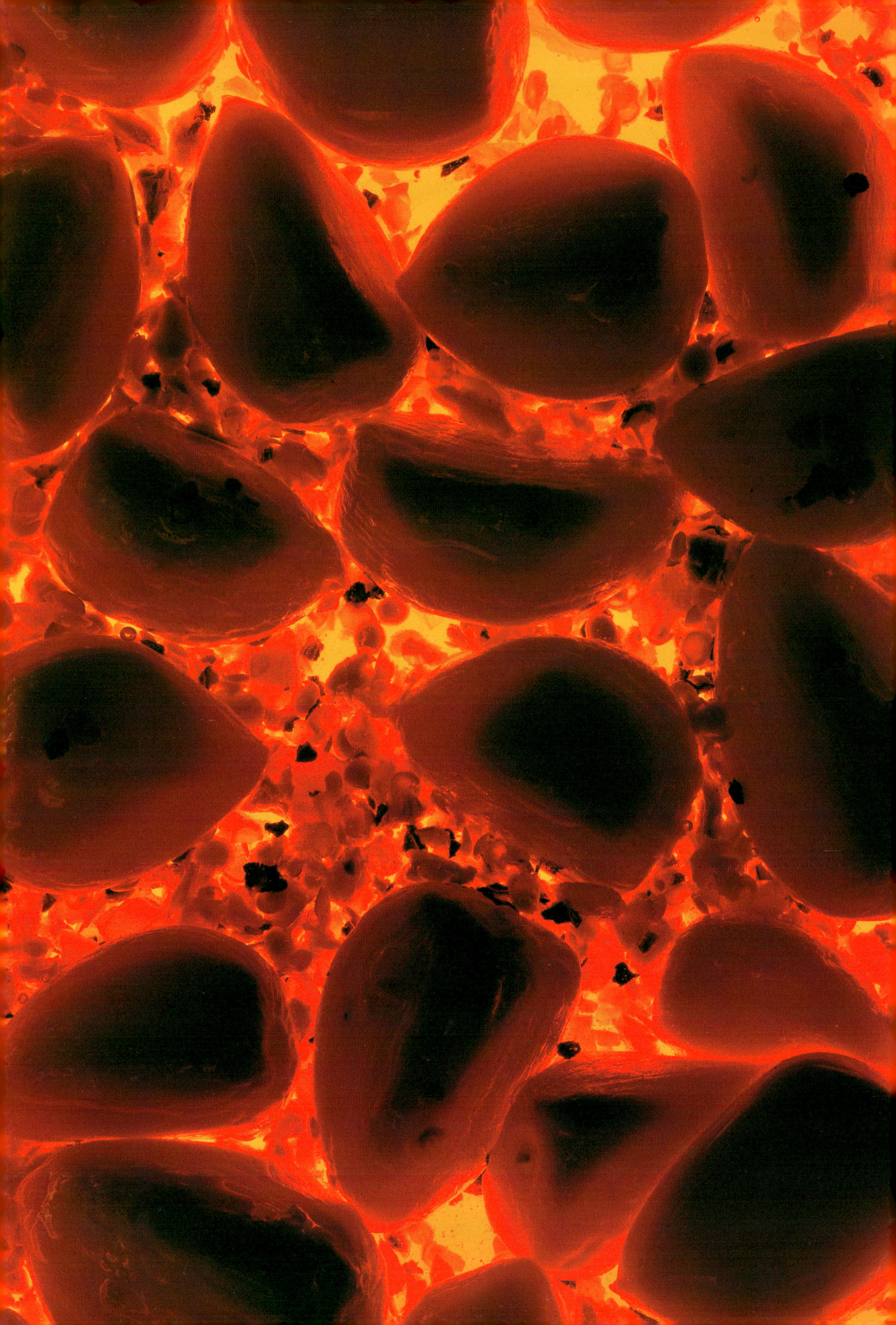

Sambal kemiri

This sambal is used to make Soto ayam (chicken soup: recipe page 36).

Preparation
Blanch the chillies. Then crush all the ingredients in a mortar.

5 red chillies
5 roasted kemiri nuts (or macadamia nuts)
pinch of salt

Sambal kelapa

Preparation
Fry the grated coconut in a pan without oil and add the Sambal kemiri. Cut the kaffir lime leaves into thin strips and stir into the mixture.

1 handful desiccated (shredded) coconut
3 tablespoons Sambal kemiri (recipe above)
2 kaffir lime leaves

Sambal bawang putih

Preparation
Peel the garlic and chop finely to make about 2 teaspoons of chopped garlic. Mix all the ingredients together.

1–2 cloves garlic
1 teaspoon Sambal Ulek (recipe page 23)
1 tablespoon rice vinegar
pinch of sugar

Anything can be preserved, from fruit and vegetables to garlic and nutmeg.

Acar: relishes

In Indonesia all dishes are served with relishes of preserved fruit or vegetables such as Acar timun (pickled gherkins), Acar lobak (pickled radishes), Acar bawang (pickled shallots), Acar kuning (pickled carrots, red shallots, chillies, cauliflower, gherkins and so on, seasoned with turmeric, garlic and other spices.). Fruit is also pickled. Sour fruit varieties such as unripe mangoes, karambola, kedondong or salak, well-known in Bali, are preserved in a sweet-and-sour pickle. Sweet fruit varieties such as jackfruit, palm fruit, sweet mangoes, lychees and rambutans are preserved in sugar only and served as a dessert.

Acar kuning

Yellow-coloured relish

2–3 carrots
1 cucumber
1 small cauliflower
20–25 fresh pickling (button) onions, or red shallots
2–3 red chillies
1 handful baby corn cobs
3 Chinese shallots
2 cloves garlic
1 piece galangal root, about 2 cm/¾ in long
1 piece ginger root, about 1 cm/⅜ in long
3 kemiri nuts (or macadamia nuts)
1 teaspoon turmeric
1 teaspoon salt
1½ tablespoons sugar
½ cup water
1 cup white rice vinegar
1 tablespoon oil for frying

Preparation
Peel the carrots, remove the seeds from the gherkins and cut both into bite-sized pieces. Wash and prepare the cauliflower and divide the florets into bite-sized pieces. Peel the pickling onions. Remove the seeds from the chillies and cut diagonally into thin strips.

Peel the shallots, garlic, galangal root and ginger and puree with the kemiri nuts. Season with turmeric and salt. Fry this paste in oil, add the sugar and stir well. Add the water and rice vinegar and bring to the boil briefly. Strain the mixture and add the carrots, gherkins, cauliflower, chillies and corn cobs to the liquid. Cover and keep in a cool place for 1 to 2 days. This relish will keep for about a week in a refrigerator.

Acar terati

Pickled lotus root

Preparation

Peel the lotus root and cut into very thin slices, no more than 3 mm/⅛ in thick. Stir the sugar into the rice vinegar, add the slices of lotus root and cover. Leave to soak in the refrigerator for 1 day (it will keep for 2 to 3 days).

If lotus roots are not available, radish, mango or pineapple may be used instead, pickled in the same way.

1 lotus root
2 teaspoons sugar
250 ml/8 fl oz (1 cup) white rice vinegar

The clear liquid contained inside a coconut is coconut water. This should not be confused with coconut milk, which is made from the flesh of the coconut.

Serundeng

1 cup desiccated (shredded) coconut
5 kaffir lime leaves
1 teaspoon garlic powder
1 teaspoon ground cumin
1½ teaspoons ground turmeric
1½ teaspoons ground coriander
½–1 teaspoon salt
250 ml/8 fl oz (1 cup) tamarind water
100 g/3½ oz (1 cup) roasted, unsalted peanuts
1 tablespoon brown sugar

Preparation

Cut the kaffir lime leaves into wafer-thin strips, then mix all the ingredients together with the exception of the peanuts and sugar. Put this mixture in the wok (on a low flame because it burns easily) and fry slowly until dry, tossing and stirring continuously, until the mixture has become yellow brown. Remove from the heat and add the roasted peanuts. Finally, stir in the brown sugar.

This fried grated coconut is delicious served with rice. It is also an excellent accompaniment to Lontong and Ketupat (see page 108) but it can also be eaten with many other dishes.

Koyah kedele

Spicy-sweet soya bean (soybean) powder

Preparation

Fry the soya beans together with the lemon leaves without any oil. Stir continuously so that they do not turn brown. Alternatively the ingredients may be roasted in the oven for 25 minutes at a temperature of 160°C (325°F), Gas mark 3.

Grind the roasted beans and lemon leaves finely, add the kencur powder and season with salt and sugar. It is important to do this while the soya beans are still hot so that the spices are better absorbed. Put the mixture in the refrigerator where it will keep a long time. It can added to a wide range of rice dishes such as for instance ketan, steamed sticky rice.

1 cup yellow soya beans (soybeans)
2–4 kaffir lime leaves
½ teaspoon kencur powder
salt
sugar

Kering tempe or Kering kentang

Fried tempe or potato sticks

Preparation

Cut the tempe or peeled potatoes into thin sticks. Peel the garlic and shallots and cut into wafer-thin slices or rings and fry until crisp. Remove the seeds from the chillies, cut into very fine strips and fry. Put all the fried ingredients to one side.

Peel the galangal root and crush. Add the salam leaves, tamarind mousse, trasi, brown sugar, salt, water and oil and stir well. Fry slowly in a wok on a low heat. It is very important to keep the temperature low so that the aroma of the galangal root and salam leaves can develop properly. The water will prevent the sugar burning and ensure that it caramelises quickly. Add the fried ingredients to this spicy mixture and stir so that they are well coated.

400 g/14 oz tempe or 400 g/14 oz peeled potatoes
5 cloves garlic
7 red shallots
5 red chillies
1 piece galangal root, about 3 cm/1¼ in long
2 salam leaves (or bay leaves)
2 tablespoons tamarind mousse
1 teaspoon trasi (shrimp paste)
2 tablespoons brown sugar
pinch of salt
2–3 tablespoons water
1 tablespoon oil
oil for frying

Soups

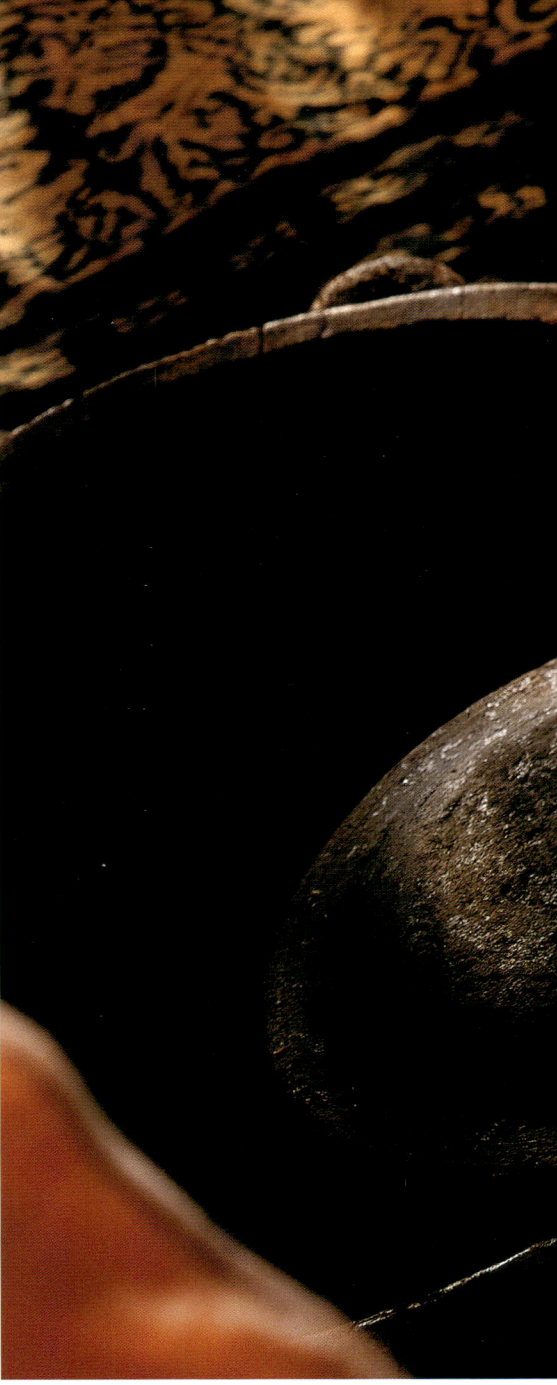

To call this section "soups" in the traditional sense is not quite correct since soups are not seen as starters (appetizers) in Indonesia, where meals are not divided into courses. Soups are usually served with other dishes, for instance, as an accompaniment to rice. However, this does not mean that Soto ayam cannot be served as a starter (appetizer) in other countries, where soup is a traditional starter.

Because stock (broth) is needed to make many of these soups, here are brief instructions for making stock yourself. To make chicken stock, simmer chicken bones and trimmings in water over a low heat for 2 hours. It is important to keep the heat low so that the stock remains clear. Do not season.

Vegetable stock is made by simmering radishes, radish skins and yellow soya beans gently over a low flame.

To make beef stock, simmer beef bones and meat slowly over a low heat. In this case whole black peppercorns and some onion skins are added. To make fish stock, simmer fish bones and trimmings with some lemon grass or a piece of ginger about 2.5 cm/1 in long.

Soto ayam

Chicken soup with traditional spices

Quantities for 4–6 people:
- 1 boiling fowl, about 1 kg/2¼ lb
- 5 litres/8½ pints (1⅓ gallons) water
- salt, pepper, lemon juice
- 4 medium potatoes
- 250 g/9 oz mung bean noodles
- 250 g/9 oz soya bean (soybean) sprouts
- 250 g/9 oz white cabbage
- 1 bunch chives
- 1 handful celery leaves

Preparation

Bring the water to the boil, add the chicken and reduce the heat because the water should only simmer. Cook the chicken for about 1½ hours. Take the chicken out of the water, remove the skin, take the meat off the bones and tear into thin strips. Peel the potatoes and boil or fry.

Prepare the ingredients for the seasoning. First crush the lemon grass, ginger and galangal root and chop the onions and garlic finely. Then puree all the ingredients in a blender. Heat the groundnut oil in a pan and add the spice mixture. Stir

continuously until all the ingredients have amalgamated. Now add this "fried" mixture to the chicken broth and season with salt, pepper and lemon juice.

Next soak the mung bean noodles in hot water. Wash the soya bean sprouts, cut the white cabbage into thin strips and wash also. Wash the celery leaves and chives and chop finely. Cut the cooked potatoes into thin slices and put on the plates. Place the mung bean noodles, soya bean sprouts, strips of raw white cabbage, strips of chicken, 2 or 3 slices of hard-boiled egg, chopped celery leaves and chives and fried onions on top. Finally pour the hot broth on top and serve immediately.

Soto ayam is often served with Sambal kemiri (recipe page 31).

The soup may also be a complete meal if served with Longton (rice in banana leaves: recipe page 108).

2 hard-boiled (hard-cooked) eggs
1 handful roasted onions

For the spicy soup seasoning:
2 sprigs lemon grass
1 piece each ginger root and galangal root, about 3 cm/1¼ in long
1 large onion or 5 shallots
3 cloves garlic
9 kemiri nuts (or macadamia nuts)
1 teaspoon ground coriander
pinch of cumin
5 kaffir lime leaves
1 teaspoon turmeric
3 tablespoons groundnut oil

Sop tahu, kentang isi

Soup with stuffed tofu (bean curd) and stuffed potatoes

Quantities for 4 people:
- 1 bunch chives
- 250 g/9 oz raw prawns or shrimps
- 1 egg
- 1 large potato
- 250 g/9 oz tofu (bean curd)
- 1.5 litres/2¾ pints (7 cups) chicken stock (broth)
- 1 handful fresh spinach
- about 20 sugar peas
- 10 dried black fungus mushrooms
- 1 bunch spring onions (scallions)
- salt
- pepper
- pinch of sugar
- sesame oil
- oil for frying

Preparation

Clean the prawn or shrimps and chop finely. Wash the chives and chop finely. Mix the prawns or shrimps and chives together, add the raw egg and season with salt and pepper. Halve the potatoes lengthways and cut diagonally into slices 1.5 cm/½ in thick. Open up each slice without cutting it right through and spread the inside with the shellfish and chives mixture.

Now cut the tofu into slices 1.5 cm/½ in thick and cut the square slices into two triangles. Open up each triangle without cutting it right through and stuff with the prawn and chives mixture.

Fry the stuffed tofu and potatoes pieces until golden brown.

Heat the chicken stock, add the fried stuffed tofu and potato pieces and simmer for 5 to 10 minutes at most. Now add the sugar peas, spinach, black fungus mushrooms, simmer briefly and season with sugar, salt and pepper. Add a few drops of sesame oil. Finally, cut the spring onions into slices and add to the mixture.

This soup is served with Sambal cuka (recipe page 29).

Juanlo

Meat and fish stew

Quantities for 4–6 people:
- 1.5 litres/2¾ pints (7 cups) chicken stock (broth)
- 2 chicken breasts
- 150 g/5 oz monkfish or salmon fillet
- 8 scampi, shelled
- about 600 g/1¼ lb vegetables (sugar peas, broccoli, cauliflower florets, courgettes (zucchini), carrots, black fungus mushrooms, rice straw mushrooms (or champignons)
- 1 bunch spring onions (scallions)
- salt, pepper
- sesame oil
- green coriander (cilantro) to taste

Preparation

Heat the chicken stock separately, seasoning with salt, pepper and sesame oil. Fillet the chicken breasts and remove the skin. Cut the chicken breasts and fish fillets into very thin slices, carpaccio-style. Clean the scampi and cut in half. Put all these ingredients in an unglazed clay pot. Cut the vegetables into bite-sized pieces, blanch and add to the pot with the other ingredients. Pour the hot stock over all. Finally, sprinkle the chopped spring onions over it. A few coriander leaves (cilantro) may be added if desired. The stew is served with soy sauce.

Tip: For a vegetarian dish, vegetable stock made from radish and soya beans may be used instead of chicken stock, while tofu can replace the meat and fish.

Tofu (bean curd) is still made in the traditional manner in this small factory.

Rawon
Spicy oxtail soup

Preparation

Bring the water to the boil. Cut the meat into cubes and add to the boiling water. Reduce the heat and cook the meat over medium heat for 1½ – 2 hours until it is tender. Add all the herbs and spices: the kaffir lime leaves, lemon grass, galangal root, salt and pepper. Then cook for a few more minutes.

Dice the tomatoes. Cut the leek onions into strips about 7 cm/3 in long, cut the chillies into thin rings. Fry the spicy soup seasoning, ground keluwek or keluwek paste, diced tomatoes, chillies and leeks in groundnut or vegetable oil until the aroma has fully developed. Season generously with salt and pepper. Add everything to the soup.

This soup is served with rice, short soya bean (soybean) sprouts, Sambal trasi (recipe page 29) and Kerupuk (page 108).

Quantities for about 5 litres/8½ pints (1⅓ gallons) for 6–8 people:
5 litres/8½ pints (1⅓ gallons) water
250 g/9 oz lean beef for soup
oxtail (4 large or 8 small pieces)
3 kaffir lime leaves
1 stem lemon grass
1 piece galangal root, about 5 cm/2 in long
salt
pepper
1 medium tomato
2 small leeks
3 tablespoons spicy soup seasoning (Soto ayam recipe page 36)
3 keluwek or 1 tablespoon keluwek paste
1 red chilli
1 tablespoon peanut or vegetable oil
salt and pepper

Samudera

Quantities for 4 people:
250 g/9 oz cooked fish, such as cod, pike or other soft-fleshed fish
about 8 mussels
1 handful dried or fresh algae (or samphire)
50 ml/1½ fl oz (3 tablespoons) rice wine
potato or tapioca flour
1 cup watercress
4 large scampi
1 piece ginger root, about 2 cm/¾ in long
salt

Clear seafood with watercress and algae

Preparation
Cut the fish into slices ½ cm/⅜ in thick and marinate for 15 minutes in white rice wine. Then sprinkle with potato or tapioca flour. Wash the watercress. Clean the scampi, mussels and algae and cut into bite-sized pieces. Blanch the fish, scampi, mussels and algae in boiling water for 2 minutes. Remove the ingredients from the water and arrange in soup bowls. Pour the fish stock into the bowls very gently so that it does not become cloudy.

This is a light fish soup with only a hint of ginger so that the flavour of the algae is not swamped. (See illustration opposite.)

Karang asem

Quantities for 4 people:
4 salmon fillets, each 50 g/2 oz
4 large scampi in shells
1 piece galangal root, about 3 cm/1¼ in long
5 cloves garlic
3 large chillies
1 stem lemon grass
2 tomatoes
1–2 tablespoons kecap manis (sweet soy sauce)
salt and pepper
2–3 tablespoons red rice vinegar
1.5 litres/2¾ pints (7 cups) water
5 shallots
1 tablespoon fish sauce

Sour-spicy fish soup

Preparation
Grill the unpeeled shallots, galangal root, cloves of garlic, chillies, tomatoes and lemon grass until slightly brown.

Then put in boiling water, season with salt, pepper, red vinegar and kecap manis and boil for 30 to 45 minutes and strain.

Clean the scampi, cut them in half and add to the strained fish stock together with the cleaned fish. Simmer for a few minutes. Serve with sambal petis (recipe page 26).

Poultry dishes

Bèbèk panggang

Roast duck

Preparation

Clean and wash the duck thoroughly and blanch in boiling salted water for about 2 minutes. Cut the lemon grass into three or four pieces, peel the ginger and cut into thin slices, peel the cloves of garlic and add to the star anise, lemon juice, coriander, cumin, cinnamon and pepper. Stuff the duck with this mixture and close the opening with bundles of wooden twigs. Leave to air-dry for about 24 hours. The following day mix together all the ingredients for the marinade and preheat the oven at its maximum setting. Place the duck on a rack with a roasting tray underneath and reduce the heat to 200°C (400°F), Gas mark 6. Cook in the oven for 1½ hours, basting regularly with marinade. (See illustration opposite.)

Quantities for 4 people:
1 duck of about 2 kg/4½ lb
1 stem lemon grass
1 piece ginger root, 2 cm/¾ in long
3–5 star anis
lime juice
1 tablespoon ground coriander
1 teaspoon cumin seeds
1 cinnamon stick
pinch of pepper
1 large clove garlic
salt

For the marinade glaze:
1 tablespoon honey
1 tablespoon soy sauce
1 tablespoon Sambal Ulek (recipe page 23)
1 tablespoon kecap manis (sweet soy sauce)
1 tablespoon oil

Bacang burung dara

Quail bacang

Preparation

Soak the sticky rice overnight. Cut the giblets into small pieces. Peel the shallots and garlic and chop finely. Cut the spring onions into pieces 1 cm/⅜ in long. Cut the shiitake mushrooms in half or quarters. Heat a few tablespoons of groundnut oil over medium heat, add the garlic and shallots and sweat until transparent. Then add the spring onions and star anise. Next add the giblets and shiitake mushrooms, cashew nuts and soya beans little by little, finishing with the sticky rice. Braise the mixture for about 10 minutes. Meanwhile preheat the oven to 180°C (350°F), Gas mark 4.

Season the quails with salt and pepper and stuff with the lightly braised mixture. Close the openings and roast the quails in the oven for about 15 minutes until ready, basting regularly with a mixture of chilli oil, sesame oil and honey.

Quantities for 4 people:
4 quails with livers and giblets
1 cup sticky rice (soak overnight)
1 handful roasted cashew nuts
3 shallots
2 cloves garlic
3 spring onions (scallions)
1 handful shiitake mushrooms
2 star anis or 2 teaspoons five-spice powder
1 tablespoon soy sauce
2–3 drops sesame oil
2–3 drops chilli oil
1 teaspoon honey to taste
pepper, salt
groundnut oil for frying

Quantities for 4 people:
2 poussins
Chinese chives or small leeks for garnish

For the sauce:
2 macadamia nuts
2 shallots
1 stem lemon grass
2 cloves garlic
1 tablespoon macadamia nut oil
2 slices fresh pineapple
5 tablespoons coconut cream
pinch of turmeric or saffron
½ vanilla pod
honey to taste

For the marinade:
½ teaspoon turmeric (for the colour)
1 tablespoon coconut milk
½ cup water
juice of ½–1 lime
salt

Kleting kuning

Poussin in pineapple and coconut sauce

Preparation

Mix all the ingredients for the marinade, stir well and rub all over the poussins. Leave them to stand for 15 to 20 minutes. Then steam the quails for about 15 to 20 minutes, in a bamboo steamer if possible. While the poussins are cooking prepare the sauce as follows. Grind the nuts finely and cut the shallots into small cubes. Cut nine thin slices from the middle section of a stalk of lemon grass. Peel the two cloves of garlic and chop finely. Sweat all these ingredients in the oil until transparent; the oil should not be preheated.

Peel and puree the pineapple. Add this to the sauce just prepared, stir well and then add the coconut cream, turmeric or saffron. Simmer for about 5 minutes. Stir in the vanilla. Cut the poussins in half, place them in the sauce and simmer for another 5 minutes. Garnish the poussin halves with leeks cut into diamond shapes or finely chopped Chinese chives. This dish is delicious served with steamed sticky rice with grated coconut.

Gudeg

Mild chicken curry with jackfruit

The main street Jl Malioboro in Yogyakarta is famous for its stalls selling gudeg – chicken with jackfruit and coconut milk. The recipe below is a simplified version.

Preparation

Crush the kemiri nuts in a mortar. Peel the garlic and shallots and also crush in the mortar. Peel the galangal root and crush. Then mix all these ingredients with the rest of the seasoning (coriander, cumin, trasi, palm sugar, salam leaves and jati leaf: the latter gives the dish a reddish colour) and stir well. Fry this mixture in groundnut oil. Cut the chicken into eight pieces and add to the fried spice mixture. Pour in the coconut milk and simmer over a low heat for about 30 minutes. When the chicken is cooked, add the jackfruit from the tin and the hard-boiled eggs. Simmer for a further 14 minutes.

Gudeg is served with Nasi liwet (recipe page 101) and Sambal bajak (recipe page 23).

Quantities for 4–6 people:
- 1 roast chicken, about 1.2 kg/2½ lb
- 4 kemiri nuts (or macadamia nuts)
- 5 cloves garlic
- 9 shallots
- 1 piece galangal root, about 2 cm/¾ in long
- 1 teaspoon ground coriander
- ½ teaspoon cumin
- 1 teaspoon palm sugar
- 2–3 salam leaves (or bay leaves)
- ½ teaspoon trasi (shrimp paste)
- 1 jati leaf
- 1 tablespoon groundnut oil
- 2 cups coconut milk
- 4 hard-boiled (hard-cooked) eggs
- 1 can young jack fruit, about 550 g/19 oz

Semur ayam tomato

Chicken stew with tomatoes

Preparation

Cut the chicken into ten pieces. Peel the shallots and garlic and cut into thin slices. Cut the tomatoes into four. Fry the shallots and garlic in the oil or butter until golden brown. Add the pieces of chicken and fry them too until golden brown. Mix the remaining ingredients with the chicken stock and pour little by little over the fried chicken mixture. Simmer for 30 to 40 minutes.

Quantities for 4–6 people:
- 1 roast chicken, 1–1.3 kg/2¼–2¾lb
- 8 shallots
- 4 cloves garlic
- 5 medium tomatoes
- 2 cloves
- about ¼ grated nutmeg
- 1 cinnamon stick
- 5 tablespoons sweet soy sauce
- 5 tablespoons soy sauce
- 1 piece ginger root, 2 cm/¾ in long
- pepper
- 4 cups chicken stock (broth)
- 4 tablespoons oil or similar amount of butter

Ayam goreng Mbok Berek

Fried chicken à la Madame Berek

Quantities for 4 people:
1 chicken, about 1.3 kg/2¾ lb
5 large shallots
2 cloves garlic
1 piece galangal root, about 2 cm/¾ in long
2–3 salam leaves (or bay leaves)
500 ml/17 fl oz (2¼ cups) coconut water
1–2 teaspoons palm sugar
salt

This dish originates from central Java and has been named after its creator.

Preparation

Peel and puree the shallots and garlic. Peel and crush the galangal root. Cut the chicken into four pieces and put in a saucepan with the coconut water (the clear liquid inside the coconut). Season and bring to the boil. Cook over medium heat until the spices cling to the chicken. Remove from the pan and fry in plenty of oil until golden brown.

This dish is delicious served with steamed rice, Sambal bajak (recipe page 23) or Sambal manis (recipe page 28) and sliced raw gherkins.

Laksa kemuning

Yellow chicken curry with rice noodles

Quantities for 4 people:
250 g/9 oz rice noodles
500 g/18 oz chicken breast fillets
12 quails' eggs
2 nutmeg flowers
1 stem lemon grass
1 cinnamon stick
1 cardamom pod
1 tablespoon oil, preferably groundnut or coconut
1 handful lemon basil (or lemon balm and basil)
1 handful shallots
250 ml/8 fl oz (1 cup) coconut milk
125 ml/4 fl oz (½ cup) chicken stock (broth)
salt, pepper

Preparation

Soak the rice noodles for a good 5 minutes in hot water. Cut the chicken breasts into thin slices. Then make the spicy paste as follows. Peel the shallots and cloves and crush with the kemiri nuts, trasi, turmeric and lime juice in a mortar to make a paste or puree in a blender.

Fry the paste in the oil together with the nutmeg flowers, lemon grass, cinnamon and the crushed cardamom pod until the mixture develops an aromatic fragrance. Add the chicken slices and fry briefly. Finally add the chicken stock and coconut milk and simmer for 10 to 15 minutes. Add the cooked, shelled quail's eggs and lemon basil. Season with salt and pepper and serve with rice noodles. Sprinkle with fried onions.

Laksa Kemuning

Ayam bumbu ruiak

Chicken in ruiak sauce

Quantities for 4 people:
1 chicken, about 1.2 kg/2½ lb
3 medium shallots
2 cloves garlic
1 piece ginger root, 1 cm/⅜ in long
5 kemiri nuts (or macadamia nuts)
3 kaffir lime leaves
1 tablespoon tomato purée
1–2 teaspoons palm sugar
salt
1 can coconut milk, about 400–500 ml/14–17 fl oz (1¾–2¼ cups)
2 tablespoons oil

Preparation
Peel the shallots and garlic and chop coarsely. Peel and chop the ginger and add together with the shallots and garlic to the kemiri nuts, lemon leaves, palm sugar and tomato puree. Season with salt and puree. Fry this paste in oil and add the chicken, frying until golden brown all over.

Now pour in the coconut milk and reduce the liquid until a thick sauce is obtained. The chicken needs to cook for 40-45 minutes.

Tip: This dish will taste even nicer if the chicken is partly cooked on a charcoal fire before frying it in the spicy paste.

Opor ayam

Chicken in coconut and curry sauce

Preparation

Peel the shallots and garlic and grind with the kemiri nuts. Add the ground coriander and cumin. Cut the chicken into four pieces and fry in oil with the shallot, garlic and nut mixture. Be careful: it must not be allowed to go brown. Crush the lemon grass and peeled galangal root. Peel the sour fruit and cut into small pieces. Next add the coconut milk, lemon grass, galangal, salam leaves and pieces of fruit. Season with salt and white pepper and cook the chicken until tender. It is best to use a clay pot and cook the chicken in the oven at a temperature of 180°C (350°F), Gas mark 4. The coconut milk thickens into a creamy sauce. Finally, season with white pepper and salt.

Quantities for 4 people:
1 chicken, 1–1.3 kg/2¼–2¾ lb
7 shallots
3 cloves garlic
4–5 kemiri nuts (or macadamia nuts)
1 teaspoon ground coriander
½ teaspoon cumin
1 stem lemon grass
1 piece galangal root,
   2 cm/¾ in long
1–2 tablespoons oil
2 belimbing wuluh (sour fruit), or
   carambola (star fruit) or rhubarb
2–3 salam leaves (or bay leaves)
750 ml/1¼ pints (3½ cups) coconut
   milk
salt
white pepper

Semur giring bèbèk

Quantities for 6 people:
1 duck, about 1.9 kg/4¼ lb
5 cloves garlic
7 shallots
1 red chillies
1 piece ginger root, about 5 cm/2 in long
1 pomegranate
1 banana flower
½ teaspoon ground coriander
1 teaspoon ground cumin
3 nutmeg flowers

Braised duck with banana flowers and pomegranate

Preparation
Clean the duck, cut off the ends of the wings and remove the breastbones. Put the bones to one side. Peel the garlic and shallots and cut into quarters (leaving one or two shallots whole). Cut the chillies into thin slices, peel and crush the ginger. Peel the remaining shallots and cut into thin rings. Cut the pomegranate in half and press one half. Peal off the petals of the banana flowers, in the same way as a globe artichoke is eaten. Next fry the quartered shallots and garlic in oil until golden brown, then add the remaining dry ingredients (chillies, coriander, cumin, nutmeg,

pepper, star anise, cinnamon, orange peel, ginger root, galangal root) and continue frying.

Stuff the duck with the fried mixture and close the opening. Roast the duck in a roasting tin for about 1 hour in the oven preheated to 200°C (400°F), Gas mark 6. Meanwhile boil the reserved duck bones in water until the liquid is sufficiently reduced. Remove the bones and strain the stock. Pour the stock into a bowl and add the soy sauce, vinegar and juice of half a pomegranate.

After cooking for an hour, add the seasoned stock and rice wine to the duck in the roasting tin, together with the banana flower petals. Roast the duck in the oven for a further 30 minutes until tender (test with a fork). Finally add the pips of half a pomegranate to the sauce. Garnish with the shallot rings.

1 teaspoon pepper
2 star anis
1 stick cinnamon
2–3 slices dried orange peel
1 piece galangal root, about 5 cm/2 in long
2 tablespoons soy sauce
1 cup duck stock (broth) from the cooked duck
1 tablespoon kecap manis (sweet soy sauce)
1 tablespoon black rice vinegar, (or balsamic vinegar)
125–250 ml/4–8 fl oz (½–1 cup) rice wine
5 tablespoons oil

Ayam goreng ijo

"Green chicken"

Preparation

Cut the chicken into 12 pieces, season with salt, sprinkle with rice flour and fry or deep-fry in oil until golden brown and crisp.

Cut the limes and green tomatoes into thin slices, cut the lemon grass diagonally into pieces 1 cm/⅜ in long and cut the chillies into thin slices. Peel the garlic and chop. Cut the kaffir lime leaves into thin strips.

Fry the garlic in oil until golden brown and add the remaining ingredients and the previously fried chicken pieces, turning them several times. Season with salt, pepper and lime juice. Sprinkle with sugar which will add a slightly caramelised taste to the dish.

Quantities for 4 people:
1 roast chicken, 1–1.2 kg/2¼–2½ lb, or about 700 g/1½ lb chicken breast fillets (2 whole breasts or fillets)
rice flour to coat the chicken pieces
1 lime
1 stem lemon grass
2 green chillies
2 spring onions (scallions)
3 cloves garlic
2 kaffir lime leaves
2–3 green tomatoes
lime juice
about 1 teaspoon sugar
salt, pepper
oil for frying

Banana flowers

Bèbèk tutu (Bèbèk Betutu)

Duck à la Betutu

Quantities for 6 people:
1 duck, about 1.9 kg/4¼ lb
5 cloves garlic
1 piece ginger root,
 about 4 cm/1½ in long
1 piece galangal root,
 about 4 cm/1½ in long
12 shallots

Besides Babi guling, Bèbèk tutu or Bèbèk Betutu (Betutu is the name of a place in Bali) is one of the best-known Balinese national dishes. For this dish, the duck is traditionally cooked on a fire of rice straw.

Preparation
Clean the duck thoroughly. Coarsely chop the garlic, ginger and galangal root. Grind the shallots, kemiri nuts, ginger and chillies together with turmeric, trasi, salt and pepper to make a paste.

Rub the duck with this paste inside and out (using half the paste), lightly massaging it into the skin and flesh. Stuff the duck with the garlic, ginger, galangal root, lemon grass and lemon leaves. Wrap the duck in a banana leaf and steam for about 30 minutes. Preheat the oven to 180°C (350°F), Gas mark 4. Open the banana leaf and rub more paste onto the duck. This time do not close the banana leaf completely. Put the duck in the preheated oven and cook for about 45 minutes at a temperature of 200°C (400°F), Gas mark 6. It may be necessary to open the banana leaf a little more to allow the duck to acquire a beautiful brown colour.

Tip: Instead of a banana leaf, which adds a subtle aroma to the dish, aluminium foil can be used.

5 kemiri nuts (or macadamia nuts)
5 red chillies

1 teaspoon turmeric
½ teaspoon trasi (shrimp paste)
1 stem lemon grass
7 kaffir lime leaves
1 teaspoon coriander
salt, pepper

Meat dishes and sate

Although Indonesia is officially a Muslim country, pork is still eaten in Bali, which is Hindu and therefore does not forbid the consumption of pork in all its variations. Thus the Balinese dish, Babi guling (sucking pig) is often served with home-made black pudding and could almost be considered the national dish of the island. On the other islands the dishes are mainly based on lamb or beef. This includes dried meat such as *dèndèng*, spicy dried beef cut into very thin slices, and *abon*, spicy, baked dry fibrous meat. Crisp beef skin, called *kerupuk rambak* or *kerupuk ulit*, is also very popular, as are grilled or fried giblets.

Street stalls and small snack bars often offer a plate of rice with stock with only a few pieces of meat so that the customer can decide what kind of meat to have with the rice: probably giblets such as beef heart, pieces of liver and so on.

MEAT DISHES AND SATE | 55

Here a few dishes are suggested that are not too difficult to prepare, and which reflect the great variety of Indonesian cuisine and taste.

Iga babi panggang
Glazed pork chops

Quantities for 4 people:
2 kg/4½ lb pork spareribs

Preparation
Whisk all the ingredients for the marinade together. Marinade the pork chops in this mixture overnight. Preheat the oven to the highest temperature. Take the chops out of the marinade, place on a rack with a roasting tin underneath and cook for about 30 minutes at a temperature of 200°C (400°F), Gas mark 6. Baste regularly with the remaining marinade (see illustration opposite). The dish is very delicious served with pak choi, soya bean (soybean) sprouts or Swiss chard and white rice.

For the marinade
1 tablespoon sesame oil
1 tablespoon hoisin sauce
1 tablespoon honey
125 ml/4 fl oz (½ cup) sherry
1 tablespoon kecap manis (sweet soy sauce)
1 tablespoon soy sauce
1 teaspoon five-spice powder
salt
coarsely ground pepper

Cèlèng brem
Wild boar in red rice wine

A rather unexpected dish in Indonesia! Wild boar is often prepared after a successful hunting expedition.

Preparation
Cut the meat into cubes. Chop the onions coarsely. Crush the garlic and galangal root separately. Cut the leeks diagonally into pieces 2 cm/3/4 in long. Fry the crushed garlic in the hot fat until golden brown. Add the chopped onion and sweat until transparent. Add the meat and brown in the lard, then add the galangal root and cloves.

When the meat is well browned, add the stock, reduce the heat and continue cooking gently for 2 to 3 hours until tender. Season with nutmeg, salt and coarsely ground pepper and simmer for a little longer. Finally add the leeks and cook for another 2 to 3 minutes and serve. It is delicious served with white rice.

Quantities for 4–6 people:
800 g/1¾ lb wild boar (or pork joint)
1 large onion
5 cloves garlic
1 piece galangal root, about 2 cm/¾ in long
1 leek
1 cup brem bali (Indonesian rice wine) (or medium port wine)
pinch of ground cloves or 2 cloves
pinch of nutmeg
salt and coarsely ground pepper
1 tablespoon pork fat for frying
2 cups meat stock (broth)

Dried beef

Daging bumbu dèndèng

Beef with coriander seeds

Quantities for 2–4 people:
500 g/18 oz beef fillet or rump
pepper

For the marinade:
3 cloves garlic
1 piece galangal root, 2 cm/¾ in long
1 tablespoon palm sugar (or
brown sugar)
1 tablespoon groundnut oil
1 tablespoon coarse ground coriander
oil for frying

For the sauce:
1 tablespoon soy sauce
1 tablespoon kecap manis (sweet
   soy sauce)
1 teaspoon Sambal ulek (recipe page
   23)
juice of ½ lemon
1 tablespoon tamarind mousse

This dish requires the meat to be cooked quickly, as does daging bawang (opposite page). This method of cooking is called "cah", meaning to sauté. Sauté dishes do not always have to be served in a thick creamy sauce as they often are in Asian restaurants in Europe. This is merely done to adapt it to non-oriental tastes. Indeed, few Asian dishes are served with a thick sauce.

Preparation
Cut the beef into very thin slices about 2 mm/³⁄₃₂ in thick (slightly thicker than for carpaccio). It is best to freeze the meat first because this makes it much easier to cut into thin slices.

Crush the garlic, grate the galangal root and mix with the sugar, groundnut oil and coriander. Put the beef slices in this mixture and turn them over so that are thoroughly coated. Leave to stand for 3 hours.

Heat the oil in a large pan. Fry the slices one by one very briefly on both sides, tossing the pan, and season with pepper. Arrange the meat on plates, stir the ingredients for the sauce briefly into the remaining cooking juices and pour over the meat. The dish goes very well with Nasi goreng (recipe page 106).

Daging bawang

Beef with red shallots and Chinese chives

Preparation

Add the chilli oil, pink peppercorns and soya sauce to the rice wine to make a marinade. Cut the meat into slices about 2 mm/$3/32$ in thick (slightly thicker than carpaccio) – it is best to freeze the meat first – and put the meat in the marinade.

Halve some of the shallots, leaving the rest whole. Cut the Chinese chives or wild garlic into pieces about 5 cm/2 in long. Heat the chilli oil in a pan or wok. Sweat the shallots until transparent and add the meat in small amounts, frying briskly on both sides, tossing the pan or wok regularly while sprinkling the oyster sauce on top. Finally stir in the chives. Serve with white rice.

Quantities for 2–3 people:
500 g/18 oz beef rump
15 small red shallots
1 bunch Chinese chives (or wild garlic)
2 tablespoons oyster sauce
1 tablespoon chilli oil for frying

For the marinade:
1 tablespoon chilli oil
1 teaspoon ground pink pepper
1 tablespoon soy sauce
50 ml/1½ fl oz (3 tablespoons) dry rice wine (or sherry)

Kambing merica

Lamb fillet with green pepper sauce

Quantities for 2–4 people:
500 g/18 oz lamb fillet
1 cup coconut milk
1 shallot
3 cloves garlic
pinch of sugar
2 tablespoons green pepper from a jar, or if available 3 sprigs fresh green pepper
up to ¼ teaspoon ground dried green pepper
1 sprig mint
1 small sprig lemon balm
1 tablespoon tamarind mousse
salt
oil for frying

Preparation

Cut the lamb fillet into thin slices, peel the shallots and cut into fine rings, peel the garlic and chop finely. Remove the mint and basil leaves from the stalks and puree.

Fry the chopped garlic in oil until golden brown. Add the shallot rings and fry until brown. Next add the meat and fry gently while tossing regularly. Pour in the coconut milk and add all the remaining ingredients, stirring continuously (if using fresh green pepper, keep one twig for the garnish). Season with salt, sugar and freshly ground green pepper.

Rayuan pulau kelapa

Delicacies from the coconut islands

Quantities for 2–3 people (about 15 sate skewers):
1 kg/2¼ lb lamb fillet or 20 very thin lamb cutlets
100 g/3½ oz desiccated (shredded) coconut

For the marinade:
2 cloves garlic
2 kaffir lime leaves
1 cup coconut milk
½ teaspoon turmeric
½ teaspoon ground coriander
1 teaspoon cumin
salt
black pepper

Any one who has been to Indonesia is familiar with sate: delicious little kebabs or brochettes, made from pieces of grilled marinated pork, beef, chicken or scampi, served with peanut and soy sauce.

Preparation

Crush the garlic, cut the kaffir lime leaves into very fine strips and add both to the other ingredients for the marinade. Stir well.

Cut the lamb into pieces about 2 cm/3/4 in by 1½ cm/⅝ in. Leave to stand in the marinade for about 30 minutes. Then thread four to five pieces on each wooden skewer. Place the kebabs or brochettes on a charcoal grill and cook over a medium heat for about 5 minutes in all, turning the kebabs frequently. Meanwhile, mix the half the remaining marinade with the grated coconut which acquires a beautiful yellow colour as a result. Remove the kebabs from the grill and roll them in the marinade with the grated coconut. Return to the grill and cook for another 1 or 2 minutes so that the grated coconut turns golden brown.

This dish can also be prepared in the oven at a temperature of 220°C (425°F), Gas mark 7. Put the kebabs in the preheated oven on a rack. Turn after 2 to 3 minutes and cook for a further 2 minutes. Remove from the oven, roll in the marinade with the grated coconut and cook for a final 1 or 2 minutes until golden brown.

These are delicious served with salad.

Tip: Depending on the number of side dishes and the appetite of your guests, reckon on three to five sate kebabs per person. As an alternative, the lamb chops can be cooked whole, without being threaded on sticks.

MEAT DISHES AND SATE | 61

Sate wangi

Aromatic sate

Quantities for 2–4 people:
about 500 g/18 oz chicken breast fillets or beef fillet
5 tablespoons groundnut oil
salt, pepper
bamboo skewers or lemon grass stems

For the marinade:
7 shallots
1 stem lemon grass
3 kaffir lime leaves
2 teaspoons coriander
½ teaspoon cumin
1 tablespoon palm sugar (or brown sugar)

For the sauce:
3 cloves garlic
100 g/3½ oz (1 cup) unsalted peanuts
250 ml/8 fl oz (1 cup) coconut milk
1 teaspoon Sambal ulek (recipe page 23)
2 tablespoons brown sugar
2 kaffir lime leaves
2–3 tablespoons kecap manis (sweet soy sauce)
juice of 1 lemon
salt

For garnishing:
kecap manis (sweet soy sauce)
shallot rings

Sate wangi is delicious served with relishes, such as Pickled lotus root (recipe page 33).
Sate is ideal for a beach picnic (see illustration on opposite page).

Preparation

Puree all the ingredients for the marinade in a blender. Cut the meat into cubes of 2 cm/¾ in, season with salt and pepper and marinate for 2 to 3 hours.

To make the peanut sauce, peel the garlic and grind together with the peanuts. Put into a saucepan with the other ingredients and simmer, stirring continuously, until the mixture has thickened sufficiently. Season with kecap manis. If the sauce is too thick, it can be thinned by adding some water. Thread five pieces of meat on each wooden or bamboo stick and grill.

If using the oven, preheat it to 220°C (425°F), Gas mark 7 and place the kebabs on a rack. Cook for 2 to 3 minutes on each side. Sprinkle kecap manis on the peanut sauce and garnish with shallot rings before serving.

Sate lilit sampi

Balinese minced beef sate

Preparation

Stir together the grated coconut and coconut milk. Peel the shallots and cut into thin rings. Peel the garlic, galangal root and ginger root and crush. Cut the chillies into thin rings or strips (remove the seeds to make the dish less hot). Cut the lemon leaves very finely.

Fry the shallot rings lightly in the oil, then add all the other spices except for the kaffir lime leaves (garlic, galangal, ginger, turmeric, coriander, kencur, tamarind mousse, palm sugar, chillies) and continue frying.

Remove all the ingredients from the pan and add to the minced beef with the finely chopped kaffir lime leaves, grated coconut, salt and pepper and mix thoroughly. Make small balls and thread them on bamboo sticks or lemon grass stalks. Press them into an oval shape and grill on a charcoal fire and grill for 3 to 5 minutes while turning regularly.

Quantities for 12–15 skewers:
300 g/10 oz minced beef
1 handful desiccated (shredded) coconut
2 tablespoons coconut milk
5 shallots
2 cloves garlic
1 piece galangal root, 5 mm/³⁄₁₆ in long
1 piece ginger root, 5 mm/³⁄₁₆ in long
1 red chillies
5 kaffir lime leaves
½ teaspoon turmeric
½ teaspoon ground coriander
pinch of kencur
1 teaspoon palm sugar
1 teaspoon tamarind mousse
salt
pepper
1 tablespoon vegetable oil
bamboo skewers

Indonesian osso buco

Preparation
Roast the shallots, garlic and chillies whole. Fry the shin bones briefly but briskly in oil until brown all round.

Heat 5 tablespoons oil in a cast iron pan or wok. Add the tamarind mousse, meat, shallots, chillies and garlic cloves. Continue to fry on a high heat.

Add the sweet soy sauce and hot water. Reduce the heat to a medium flame. Add the salam leaves and lemon grass, cover and cook for 30 minutes. Remove the lid and cook for another 5 to 10 minutes. Season with salt and crushed jawa pepper. (See illustration opposite page.)

Quantities for 4 people:
- 4 pieces shin of beef
- 25 small sweet-and-sour shallots (preserved or bottled)
- 1½ large cloves garlic
- 3 large red chillies
- 1 tablespoon tamarind mousse
- 1 stem lemon grass
- 3 salam leaves (or bay leaves)
- 125 ml/4 fl oz (½ cup) kecap manis (sweet soy sauce)
- 500 ml/17 fl oz (2¼ cups) stock (broth) or water
- ½–1 teaspoon jawa pepper
- salt
- oil for frying

Babi cin

Pork cutlets in date and mushroom sauce

Preparation
Soak the pearl barley in water. Soak the dried dates and shiitake mushrooms. Peel the garlic and cut into thin slices. Peel the ginger and crush.

Heat the oil in a pan and fry the cutlets briskly. (In Bali belly of pork is also often used instead of cutlets.) Add the garlic and ginger and fry with the cutlets. Reduce the heat and add the sugar so that it caramelises. Add the arrak or rose schnapps, soy sauce, five-spice powder mixture and cloves and stir well. Next add the pearl barley, shiitake mushrooms and dates together with the water in which they have soaked. Season with coarsely ground black pepper and a little more soy sauce. Cover and braise for a further 15 to 20 minutes. This is a very traditional dish, served with Lontong cap goh meh èbès (see page 108).

Quantities for 4 people:
- 4 pork cutlets
- 1 handful pearl barley
- 7 dried red dates
- 7 dried shiitake mushrooms
- 2 cloves garlic
- 1 piece ginger root, about 1 cm/⅜ in long
- 1 tablespoon sugar
- 4 tablespoons soy sauce
- 2 tablespoons arrack or rose schnapps
- 2 tablespoons five-spice mixture, not ground
- 1 clove
- coarsely ground black pepper
- 1–2 tablespoons oil for searing the meat

Babi guling

Balinese sucking pig

1 sucking pig, 25–35 kg/55–75 lb

For the stuffing:
3 ginger roots
3 galangal roots
kencur root, about 8 cm/3 in long
8–10 stems lemon grass
3–4 large cloves garlic
45 shallots
35 kemiri nuts (or macadamia nuts)
25 red chillies

Traditionally, Babi guling is prepared with a small pig (the Indonesian name means "pig on a spit"), stuffed with herbs and cooked on a spit over an open fire made with wood, coconut peelings and rice straw. Originally, very young sucking pigs were used, weighing about 6 kg/13 lb, but now larger animals are also used, weighing 25–35 kg/55–75 lb. This means that the quantities must be adapted accordingly. It is served with rice and also with *lawar*, Balinese black pudding. If the dish is ordered at a Balinese food stall or snack bar, it is served on banana leaves and eaten with the fingers.

Preparation

Peel the ginger and galangal root and chop coarsely. Cut the lemon grass stalks into 3 pieces each. Peel the garlic and chop very coarsely. Peel the shallots. Coarsely puree the shallots, kemiri nuts and chillies together with the turmeric, coriander, trasi, salt and pepper to make a paste. Stuff the cleaned sucking pig with this paste together with the ginger and galangal root, kencur, lemon grass, kaffir lime leaves, salam leaves and garlic (having first rubbed the inside with this mixture). Close up the sucking pig and slide onto the spit.

Dilute the lemon or lime juice with water and season with turmeric and salt. Coat the skin of the piglet with this yellow liquid. Repeat regularly during the cooking process.

Spit-roast over an open fire for 4 to 6 hours depending on the size and stuffing of the sucking pig. Turn and baste the piglet continuously during the cooking process.

3–4 tablespoons ground turmeric
6–7 tablespoons ground coriander
2 tablespoons trasi (shrimp paste)
25–30 kaffir lime leaves
7–10 salam leaves (or bay leaves)
coarsely ground black pepper
salt, pepper

For the glaze:
about 500 ml/17 fl oz (2¼ cups) lemon or lime juice
about 250 ml/8 fl oz (1 cup) water
2–3 tablespoons ground turmeric
2 tablespoons salt

Opor kelinci gigit daun

Saddle of rabbit opor with lily flowers and green tea leaves

Preparation

Fry the rabbit bones briefly, add water and bring to the boil. Continue boiling to reduce the liquid. Throw away the bones and strain the liquid.

Soak the dried lily flowers and lotus hearts. Peel the onions and chop finely.

Fry the saddle of rabbit briskly on both sides – the outside must be seared to ensure that the meat remains tender. Season lightly with pepper and put to one side.

Sweat the chopped onion in the pan until transparent. Add the softened lily flowers and lotus hearts as well as the green tea leaves. Add a cup of the stock, bring to the boil and stir in the coconut cream. Simmer the pieces of rabbit briefly in the sauce. Season with salt and pepper.

This dish is delicious with Lontong cap meh èbes (see page 108).

Quantities for 4 people:
6–8 pieces saddle of rabbit
1 handful dried lily flowers (from oriental shops)
1 handful lotus hearts
1 white onion
1 teaspoon green tea leaves
2 tablespoons coconut cream
rabbit bones for the stock (broth)
salt
pepper
2 tablespoons oil

Fish and seafood

The culinary tradition of a country surrounded by sea would naturally be assumed to be based on fish and seafood, and it is indeed true that many Indonesians are fond of shrimps, scampi and mussels. Lavish dishes with expensive ingredients are served on special festive occasions. But for the ordinary rice farmer and poor fisherman, such exotic seafood is an unaffordable luxury. Their diet consists instead of very simple fish dishes, if the mouthwatering recipes on the following pages can be so described. Dried fish or crab paste may be the only ingredient based on fish or seafood served with the rice, or perhaps tiny little fishes cooked on a spit in the fire. In the Indonesian representation of the world of gods and people, all evil comes from the sea and the sea is part of the underworld. But in spite of this, fish and seafood are an important part of the Indonesian culinary tradition.

In the Indonesian representation of the world of gods and people, all evil comes from the sea and the sea is part of the underworld. But in spite of this, fish and seafood are an important part of the Indonesian culinary tradition.

Gulai bahari

Fish in coconut cream sauce

Quantities for 4–5 people:
- 2 red mullet or other fish suitable for boiling
- 1 large or 4–5 small squid, cleaned
- 1 piece cod
- 5 medium scampi
- 1 cup mussels
- 5–6 green mussels

- 3 cloves garlic
- 1 onion or 5 Chinese shallots
- 3 cherry tomatoes
- 1 piece galangal root, 2.5 cm/1 in long
- 1 piece ginger root, 2.5 cm/1 in long
- ½ teaspoon turmeric
- ½ teaspoon ground
- 2 teaspoons cumin
- salt and sugar to taste
- 1–2 teaspoons Sambal ulek (recipe page 23)
- 2 tablespoons oil
- 2 cloves
- 1 cardamom pod
- 1 cinnamon stick
- 2 stems lemon grass
- 2–3 kaffir lime leaves
- 200 ml/7 fl oz (⅞ cup) coconut cream
- 250 ml/8 fl oz (1 cup) fish stock (broth) or water

Preparation

To clean the red mullet, cut open lengthways on the belly side and remove the insides. Rinse thoroughly under the tap and carefully remove the scales with a blunt knife. Make three diagonal cuts on each side.

Cut each squid so as to obtain a rectangular piece. Cut this widthways into strips 3-4 cm/1–1½ in long and make cuts in their surface to create a diamond pattern. Wash the cod, mussels and scampi. Remove the intestines of the scampi by opening them up lengthways along the back. Cut the cod into cubes.

Chop the cloves of garlic. Cut the onion or shallots and the cherry tomatoes in half. Crush the galangal and ginger roots. In a mortar coarsley pound together the cloves of garlic and one half onion or five half shallots withthe turmeric, coriander, cumin, salt, sugar and sambal ulek, or puree in a blender. Be careful not to let it become like a smooth mousse.

Heat the oil in a pan over a high flame. Add the coarsely pureed mixture together with the cloves, cardamom, cinnamon, galangal root, ginger, lemon grass, kaffir lime leaves and halved tomatoes. Next add the coconut cream and the fish stock or water. Bring to the boil. Add the rest of the onions or shallots.

Finally, add the fish – the red mullet, cod and squid – and simmer over a low heat. After about 15 minutes, add the mussels and scampi and simmer for a further 5 minutes.

Serve with white rice or white sticky rice.

Ikan/udang bumbu taoco

Fish or scampi in yellow bean sauce

Preparation

Clean the fish or scampi, season with salt and pepper and sprinkle with rice flour. Fry in some oil and put to one side.

To make the spice mixture, peel the ginger and garlic and chop both finely. Peel the shallots and cut into small dice. Fry the shallots and garlic in the oil until golden brown. Add the ginger and stir in the taoco, tossing the pan. Next add the stock and then the peppercorns. Add the fish or scampi and simmer for about 5 minutes, tossing the pan now and again. Season with soy sauce and garnish with celery and coriander leaves. Serve with rice.

Quantities for 4 people:
about 800 g/1¾ lb carp fillets or scampi
1 handful celery leaves or green coriander (cilantro)
2 tablespoons kecap manis (sweet soy sauce)
salt, pepper
rice flour to coat the fish

For the seasoning:
1 piece ginger root, 1 cm/⅜ in long
3 cloves garlic
5 shallots
½ teaspoon peppercorns
2 tablespoons taoco (bean paste)
1 cup fish or shrimp stock (broth)

Brèngkès tongkol, gubis

Tuna fish parcels with Savoy cabbage

Preparation

Peel the garlic, galangal root, chillies and keluwek. Pound and mix them together. Fry the mixture with trasi in 3 tablespoons oil. Season with lemon juice and sugar.

Separate the leaves of the Savoy cabbage and blanch. Cut the fish into large cubes and roll in the fried paste so that they are well coated in it. Place these coated fish pieces on the cabbage leaves, wrap into small parcels and steam for about 15 minutes. Remove from the steam and allow to cool.

Heat some oil in a pan and fry the fish parcels gently on all sides over a low flame.

Quantities for 4 people:
500 g/18 oz tuna fish
1 Savoy cabbage
5 cloves garlic
1 piece galangal root, 2 cm/¾ in long
5 red chillies
1 keluwek (may be omitted)
1 teaspoon trasi (shrimp paste)
juice of 1 lemon
1 teaspoon palm sugar (or brown sugar)
salt
oil for frying

Ikan bumbu Bali

Red snapper in red sauce

Quantities for 4–5 people:
1 red snapper, about 1 kg/2¼ lb
10 large red chillies
5 red onions
palm sugar to taste (or brown sugar)
1 piece galangal root,
   about 2 cm/¾ in long
1 piece ginger root,
   about 5 mm/³⁄₁₆ in long
juice of ½ lime
½ teaspoon trasi (shrimp paste)
3 cloves garlic
white pepper
salt
rice flour for coating the fish

Preparation
Clean the red snapper and make several diagonal cuts on both sides. Season with salt and pepper and sprinkle with rice flour. Deep-fry (but if the pan is not large enough, you can bake the fish in the oven for about 25 minutes at 200 degrees C). Puree the chillies with a little salt in the blender to obtain a coarse mixture. Cut the red onions into thin slices, peel the ginger and galangal root and crush/pound. Add to the chilli mixture together with the trasi and lemon juice and stir well. Peel and crush the cloves of garlic, fry in some oil, add to the chilli-trasi mixture and simmer for about 10 minutes until the onions are transparent. Place the fish in the sauce, turning it to make sure it is coated all round, and serve. Serve with fresh cucumber slices, rice and kerupuk.

Tip: If this dish is served with several others, the fish may be replaced with eggs. Reckon on one egg (cut in half) per person. The eggs are first hard-boiled (hard-cooked), then deep fried. The rest of the recipe remains the same, except that the quantities should be halved.

Other variations:
Small sardines or fresh anchovies are a delicious addition to this recipe.
Strict vegetarians or vegans can use tempe and/or potatoes, pre-boiled and then deep fried.

Kakap goreng kecap

Sea bass in black sauce

Quantities for 4–5 people:
- 1 sea bass, about 1 kg/2¼ lb)
- 3 cloves garlic
- 2 red onions
- 1 cinnamon stick
- 2–3 nutmeg flowers
- **palm sugar to taste, (or brown sugar)**
- 1 piece ginger root, about 2 cm/¾ in long
- 1 level teaspoons petis
- 1 tablespoon soy sauce
- 125 ml/4 fl oz (½ cup) kecap manis (sweet soy sauce)
- 100 ml/3½ fl oz (½ cup) fish stock (broth)
- 2 tablespoons palm wine
- juice of 1 lime
- salt
- rice flour to coat the fish

Preparation

Peel the garlic and red onions, cut into thin slices and fry briefly. Remove half the fried garlic and onion mixture. Add the cinnamon, nutmeg flowers, palm sugar, peeled and finely cut ginger root and petis and continue frying. Add the savoury and sweet soya sauces and simmer for a while. Add the fish stock and reduce the liquid. Next add the palm wine and simmer for 5-10 minutes.

Clean the sea bass thoroughly (gut and remove the scales). Make several diagonal cuts on both sides, dab dry, season with salt, sprinkle with lemon juice and dust with rice flour. Deep fry the fish whole , or if the pan is too small for the fish, bake in the oven for about 25 minutes at 200°C (400°F), Gas mark 6. Finally pour the sauce over the fish and garnish with the rest of the fried garlic and onion rings. Serve with white rice.

Sambal goreng rebung yuyu

Small crabs in bamboo and coconut sauce

Preparation

Peel the shallots and garlic and cut into thin slices. Remove the seeds from the chillies, cut into thin rings or strips and sweat with the galangal root and kaffir lime juice. As soon as the onions have become transparent, add the rest of the ingredients except for the crabs. Simmer for about 10 minutes. Finally add the crabs and simmer for a further 5 minutes. Serve with white rice.

> Tip: This type of recipe is also ideal for vegetarians. Instead of crabs, slices of tofu (bean curd) and/or tempe or beans may be used. The fish stock can be replaced by vegetable stock made from radishes, onion peel, white pumpkin (coyote) and soya beans (soybeans).

Quantities for 6 people:
800 g/1¾ lb small crabs (or crayfish)
3 shallots
3 cloves garlic
1 red and 1 green chilli
1 piece galangal root, about 5 cm/2 in long
2 salam leaves (or bay leaves)
3 kaffir lime leaves
about 100 g/3½ oz bamboo sprouts (from a can)
1 teaspoon sugar
salt to taste
1 teaspoon Sambal ulek (recipe page 23)
5 tablespoons coconut milk
pinch of trasi (shrimp paste)
½ cup fish stock (broth)

Kepiting kukus

Crab with pineapple sambal

Quantities for 1 person (1 crab per person)
1 large crab
1 stem lemon grass
1 stem leek

For the pineapple sambal:
1 clove garlic
3 slices fresh pineapple (or canned)
juice of ½ lime
1 teaspoon salt
corasely ground pepper
1 piece ginger root,
    about 5 mm/³⁄₁₆ in long

Preparation
Clean the crabs, remove the top part of the shell and stuff the crab with lemon grass and leeks. Steam until they turn bright red.

It is served with a variation of pineapple sambal (recipe page 26) that is better suited to this crab dish. To make this variation, cut the garlic into wafer-thin slices, fry in the oil and puree all the other ingredients coarsely. For extra heat, cut two small red chillies and one green one into thin slices and add. Stir the garlic and the rest of the ingredients together.

Serve with the steamed crab.

Udang pandan

Scampi with pandanus leaves

Preparation

Clean the scampi by opening lengthways along the back and removing the intestines. Cut one of the pandanus leaves into fine, wafer-thin strips.

Puree the ingredients for the spice mixture together with the second pandanus leaf, or better still crush in a mortar. Then fry this mixture in s oil together with the strips of pandanus leaf until an aromatic fragrance rises from the pan. Add the coconut milk and stir well into a smooth mixture. Simmer for 15 minutes. Next add the scampi and simmer for another 5 minutes. Season with salt and pepper. The pandanus leaves give the dish a beautiful green colour.

Quantities for 4 people:
25 scampi
2 pandanus leaves
salt and pepper to taste
250 ml/8 fl oz (1 cup) coconut milk
4 tablespoons oil for frying

For the spice mixture:
5 kemiri nuts (or macadamia nuts)
5 shallots
3 cloves garlic
2–3 pieces sugar cane about 10 cm/4 in long, or 3–5 lumps white candy sugar

Sambal goreng udang/ebi

Shrimps or crabs in Sambal goreng

Sambal goreng is a dish that is popular throughout Indonesia. This recipe is a Javanese variation of the basic recipe, using king prawns, *udang*, or crabs, *ebi*. There are several kinds of Sambal goreng with the same basic ingredient, chilli; for instance, sambal goreng buncis (with green beans), sambal goreng ati (with liver), and sambal goreng tahu (with tofu).

Preparation

Peel the manisah and cut into sticks. Cut the chillies into strips. Peel the garlic and chop finely. Peel the shallots and cut into thin slices. Heat the oil in a pan, add the garlic and shallots and fry until transparent. Next add the manisah, red chillies, trasi, galangal root, kaffir lime leaves, salam leaves and tamarind mousse. Finally add the prawns and coconut milk and stir well. Simmer for 5 minutes. If necessary, thin the sauce with fish or prawn stock (broth). Season with salt and brown sugar. This is delicious served with white rice.

Quantities for 4 people:
500 g/18 oz king prawns or crabs
1 manisah (or kohlrabi)
2 red chillies
3 cloves garlic
5 shallots
½ teaspoon trasi (shrimp paste)
1 piece galangal root, about 3 cm/1¼ in long
3 kaffir lime leaves
2 salam leaves (or bay leaves)
1 teaspoon tamarind mousse
1 cup coconut milk
125 ml/4 fl oz (½ cup) fish or shrimp stock (broth)
brown sugar and salt to taste
3 tablespoons oil for frying

Kuran banyubiru

Bream with two sauces

Quantities for 4 people:
- 1 bream or pink perch, about 800 g/1¾ lb
- about 250 g/9 oz prawns
- 1 stem lemon grass
- 125 ml/4 fl oz (½ cup) fish stock (broth) or water
- salt
- sugar

For the prawn sauce:
- 1 medium tomato
- 1 teaspoon turmeric
- 3 red chillies
- 3 kemiri nuts (or macadamia nuts)
- 1 piece ginger root, about 2 cm/¾ in long
- 5 shallots
- 3 cloves garlic
- 2 tablespoons oil for frying and oil for the fish

For the soy sauce:
- 4 red shallots
- 2 cloves garlic
- 1 cinnamon stick
- 1 teaspoon Sambal ulek (recipe page 23)
- 1 tablespoon oil for frying
- 250 ml/8 fl oz (1 cup) kecap manis (sweet soy sauce)
- mint leaves

Preparation

Clean and gut the fish. Season with salt and fry in oil till crisp. Remove from the pan. To make the prawn sauce, grind or puree all the ingredients for the sauce and fry briefly in oil with the crushed lemon grass until the mixture develops an aroma. Add the prawns to sauce and stir. Add the stock and season with salt and sugar.

To make the soya sauce, peel two shallots and the garlic, chop finely and fry in the oil. Add the cinnamon and sambal, simmer briefly, then add the soy sauce and simmer a little longer. Arrange in a dish and garnish with rest of the shallot rings and a few mint leaves.

Serve the sauces separately from the deep fried fish.

Udang nenas

Scampi with pineapple

Preparation
Cut the chillies and kaffir lime leaves into thin strips. Peel the garlic and cut into thin slices. Heat the margarine and fry the garlic in it until golden brown. Add the scampi and, shortly afterwards, all the other ingredients. Season with honey, salt and lemon juice and simmer for about 5 minutes.

Quantities for 4 people:
500 g/18 oz medium scampi, shelled
2 red chillies
3 kaffir lime leaves
5 cloves garlic
2 cups fresh pineapple chunks
75 g/3 oz pickling (button) onions
about 125 ml/4 fl oz (½ cup) pineapple juice
honey, salt, lemon juice
1 tablespoon margarine for frying

Lobster dalam tempurung

Lobster salad with coconut

Quantities for 4 people:
- 2 lobsters
- 2 young coconuts
- 1 small carambola (star fruit), still green
- green coriander (cilantro) and mint to taste
- juice of 2 limes
- Malabar pepper
- ground green pepper
- salt
- macadamia nut oil

A refreshing salad which should be enjoyed on a palm beach.

Preparation

Remove the top of each coconut and scoop out the white flesh in strips. Cut the star fruit into thin slices and remove the coriander leaves from the stalks.

Cook the lobster in boiling water until they turn red. Remove the flesh and tear into small strips.

Mix together the strips of coconut and lobster. Add the star fruit and season with lime juice, salt, pepper and macadamia nut oil. Fill the larger coconut halves with the lobster mixture and garnish with coriander leaves and mint.

Tip: Add a further decorative note by garnishing each stuffed coconut with the head and claws of the lobsters.

Tirem kukus cuka merah

Steamed oysters with red vinegar

Preparation
Clean and open the oysters. Cut the chillies into thin strips, peel the garlic, cut into slices and fry lightly in oil, peel the ginger and chop finely. Add to the celery leaves, mix well and arrange on the oysters. Add the lemon grass and kaffir lime leaves. Steam for a few minutes until tender. Garnish with finely chopped chillies, Sprinkle vinegar and soya sauce on top.

Quantities for 4 people:
12 oysters
1 red chillies
3 cloves garlic
1 piece ginger root, about 1 cm/⅜ in long
celery leaves
1 stem lemon grass
3 kaffir lime leaves
1 tablespoon red rice vinegar
1 tablespoon soy sauce
pepper
2 tablespoons oil

Mutiara

Scallops in jasmine tea

A delicious, sophisticated starter that is also a perfect side dish to serve with spicy fish soup with chives and rice.

Preparation
Clean the fish fillets and cut into eight cubes. Cut the silk tofu in 8 or 16 pieces. Soak the dried lily flowers in water. On each clean, open scallop shell, place a piece of fish, tofu, lily flower (arranging the filaments in a decorative manner), a few tea leaves with jasmine flowers and candied pumpkin . Sprinkle with tea (liquid) and a little sea-salt. Cook the scallops for about 3-5 minutes in a steamer.

Quantities for 4 people:
8 fresh scallops
2 fish fillets (whiting or flounder)
1 piece silk tofu (bean curd)
16 dried lily flowers
250 ml/8 fl oz (1 cup) green jasmine tea (made from of 1 teaspoon tea leaves and flowers)
tea leaves with jasmine flowers
8 or 16 thin pieces tangkue (candied white pumpkin)
pinch of sea salt

Dried lily flowers

Tumis kerang

Fried mussels

Quantities for 4 people:
2 kg/4½ lb mussels
5 cloves garlic
1 piece ginger root, 2 cm/¾ in long
1 stem lemon grass
1 tablespoon Sambal ulek (recipe page 23)
1 teaspoon trasi (shrimp paste)
2 tablespoons kecap manis (sweet soy sauce)
1 tablespoon soy sauce or fish sauce
sesame oil
2–3 tablespoons lime juice
1 bunch chives or 3 spring onions (scallions)
salt, coarsely ground pepper
2–3 tablespoons oil

Preparation
Wash the mussels. Peel the ginger and garlic and chop finely. Crush the lemon grass. Heat the oil in the pan and fry the garlic until light brown, then add the ginger and lemon grass to the pan and fry before adding the mussels. Stir well and add the sambal, trasi, kecap manis and soya sauce little by little, stirring all the while. Sprinkle on a few drops of sesame oil and a little lime juice. Season with salt and pepper. Garnish with chopped chives or spring onions.

Ikan tim rumput laut

Steamed fish with seaweed

Quantities for 2 people:
500 g/18 oz turbot or skate wing
sesame oil
1 handful seaweed or algae
1 piece ginger root, about 1 cm/⅜ in long
1 tablespoon taosi (bean paste)
3 tablespoons rice wine
salt, pepper
leak strips and green coriander (cilantro) for garnish
oil for frying

Preparation
Remove the bones and cut the fish into cubes. Peel the ginger and cut into thin sticks. Fry the pieces of fish in the oil, remove from the pan and arrange on a plate. Sprinkle with sesame oil, salt, pepper, seaweed, strips of ginger and taosi. Add the rice wine and steam for 15 minutes until cooked.

Garnish with strips of leek and coriander leaves just before serving.

FISH AND SEAFOOD | 83

Quantities for 4 people:
500 g/18 oz small cleaned squid
juice of 1 lime

For the stuffing
150 g/5 oz fish fillet, such as cod
1 egg white
2 tablespoons chopped almonds
1 clove garlic
1 bunch chives
5 leaves lemon basil (or lemon balm and basil)
lime juice
pinch of nutmeg flowers
2 tablespoons coconut cream (this rises to the surface in canned coconut milk and may be used so long as the can is not shaken)
salt
pepper

Cumi cumi kenari

Squid in kumquat sauce

Preparation
To make the stuffing, chop all the ingredients coarsely – including the fish fillet – and stir in the egg white and coconut cream. Stuff the squid with this mixture. Steam for about 5 minutes and put to one side.

To make the sauce, cut the two kumquats and the candied ginger into very thin slices. Caramelise the sugar lightly and add the fish stock. Add the kumquat and ginger and season with rice vinegar, salt and lime juice. Reduce the sauce. Pour the hot sauce over the stuffed squids and garnish with chopped chives before serving.

For the sauce
2 kumquats
1 piece preserved ginger
2 tablespoons sugar
125 ml/4 fl oz (½ cup) fish stock (broth)
lime juice and red rice vinegar
salt
chives for garnish

Vegetable and tofu (bean curd) dishes

Cah kacang panjang

Sautéed asparagus beans

Preparation

Cut the tofu into cubes of 1 cm/⅜ in and cut the tempe into cubes or slices. Cut the chillies diagonally into pieces about 1 cm/⅜ in long. Crush the garlic. Wash the beans. Blanch and plunge briefly into ice cold water to maintain their beautiful fresh green colour. Then sauté them in a wok in hot groundnut or soya bean oil and arrange on a dish. Next fry the garlic, tempe, tofu and chillies in the wok, stirring continuously. Season with the fish sauce, salt, coarsely ground black pepper and a pinch of sugar. Finally add the taosi and pour this mixture over the green beans.

Quantities for 4 people:
250 g/9 oz kacang panjang (asparagus beans) or green (snap) beans)
250 g/9 oz tofu (bean curd)
250 g/9 oz tempe
2 large green chillies
5 cloves garlic
salt
coarsely ground black pepper
pinch of sugar
50 ml/1½ fl oz (3 tablespoons) kecap ikan (fish sauce; vegetarians can replace this with ordinary soy sauce)
2 tablespoons taosi
1–2 tablespoons groundnut or soya bean (soybean) oil to sauté

Gimbal mawut

Vegetable balls

Quantities for 4 people:
- 150 g/5 oz small shrimps, shelled
- 1 red chillies
- 100 g/3½ oz tofu (bean curd)
- 2–3 cloves garlic
- 2 carrots
- 1 bunch wild garlic
- 1 bunch lemon basil (or lemon balm and basil)
- 2 bunches spring onions (scallions)
- 500 g/18 oz soya bean sprouts
- 1 handful celery leaves
- 200g/7 oz (scant 2 cups) rice flour
- 200g/7 oz (scant 2 cups) wheat flour
- 2 eggs
- 150 ml/5 fl oz (⅝ cup) coconut milk
- water
- 1 teaspoon coriander
- pinch of cumin
- pinch of kencur
- salt, pepper
- up to ¼ teaspoon turmeric
- oil for frying

For the sauce:
- 5 cloves garlic
- 250 ml/8 fl oz (1 cup) kecap manis (sweet soy sauce)
- juice of 1 lemon
- 1 tablespoon Sambal ulek (recipe page 23)
- 1 teaspoon trasi (shrimp paste)
- 1 tablespoon chopped unsalted peanuts

Preparation

Clean the shrimps, cut the chillies into thin slices, dice the tofu, peel and chop the garlic. Peel the carrots and grate coarsely. Cut the wild garlic and spring onions into thin rings and chop the lemon basil. Mix the rice and wheat flour with the eggs, coconut milk and if necessary water to make a batter. Season with coriander, cumin, kencur, salt and pepper. Stir in a little turmeric (only for the colour). Add the shrimps and vegetable and mix thoroughly. Fry like pancakes in plenty of oil.

Meanwhile prepare the sauce (it may also be prepared in advance). Peel the garlic, chop and mix with the other ingredients.

Note: People who prefer their food less spicy should use a smaller quantity of Sambal ulek, perhaps only a teaspoon.

Urap urap

Mixed vegetable with coconut

Preparation
Wash all the vegetable thoroughly. Peel the kohlrabi and the cucumber and cut into sticks. Chop up the cabbage. Blanch all the vegetable except for the cucumber and drain well. Peel the cloves of garlic, crush and mix thoroughly with the other ingredients for the spicy paste. Next steam this paste for about 10 minutes. Traditionally, it is steamed in a banana leaf but aluminium foil will also work. Finally add the paste to the blanched vegetables, stir well and garnish with some lemon basil.

Quantities for 4 people:
- 2 handfuls soya bean sprouts
- 2 handful kacang panjang (asparagus beans) or green (snap) beans
- 2 handful kangkung (water spinach) (or leaf spinach)
- 1 kohlrabi
- ¼ cucumber
- ½ small Savoy cabbage
- lemon basil (or lemon balm and basil) for garnish

For the spicy paste:
- 2 cloves garlic
- 1 cup desiccated (shredded) coconut
- 1 teaspoon trasi (shrimp paste)
- 1 teaspoon Sambal ulek (recipe page 23)
- ½ teaspoon kencur
- pinch of salt, sugar

Telur puyuh petis

Quails' eggs in coconut cream

Preparation
Boil the quails' eggs for 2–3 minutes (hens' eggs for 8–9 minutes). Shell the eggs and fry half of them in oil until light brown. Cut the chillies into thin strips, peel the shallots and garlic, pound into a paste and fry together with crab paste (petis) in 2 tablespoons of oil. Crush the kunci and galangal root (peeled). Add together with the coconut milk, tamarind water, salt and sugar. Simmer over a low heat for 5 minutes. Finally add the quails' eggs and simmer briefly.

This dish is delicious served with Lontong or normal rice, as part of a rijstafel, or with Lontong cap goh meh èbès (recipe page 108).

Quantities for 4 people:
- 12 quails' eggs or 4 hens' eggs
- 1 red chilli
- 3 shallots
- 2 cloves garlic
- 1 teaspoon petis
- 1 piece kunci, about 2 cm/¾ in long
- 1 piece galangal root, about 3 cm/1¼ in long
- 2 cups coconut milk
- 1–2 tablespoons tamarind water
- salt
- pinch of sugar
- oil

Quantities for 4 people:
250 g/9 oz tofu (bean curd)
250 g/9 oz tempe
2 salam leaves (or bay leaves)
1 piece galangal root,
   about 2 cm/¾ in long
2 red chillies
2 green chillies
3 cloves garlic
5 shallots
5 tablespoons kecap manis (sweet
   soy sauce)
juice of 1 lime or tamarind water
salt
2 tablespoons oil for frying

Oseng oseng tahu tempe

Spicy fried tofu (bean curd) and tempe

A simple dish for every day which is popular in both villages and cities.

"Spicy fried tofu and tempe are popular in both villages and cities."

Preparation
Cut the tofu into cubes of 2cm/¾ in. Cut the tempe into slices of about 2 x 3 x 1 cm/¾ x 1¼ x ⅜ in. Fry both until golden brown and put to one side. Meanwhile crush the galangal root, cut the red and green chillies diagonally into pieces of about 1 cm/⅜ in, peel the garlic and shallots and cut into thin slices. Fry the garlic in the oil, add the shallots and fry until transparent. Stir in the other condiments. Then add the fried tempe and tofu and season with the sweet soy sauce and salt. Finally, add the lime juice or tamarind water.

Terong bajak

Fiery aubergines (eggplants)

Quantities for 2–4 people:
- 1 large purple aubergine (eggplant)
- 6 terong gelatik (small greenish-white aubergines)
- 250 g/9 oz chicken or shrimps
- 2 small shallots
- 2 cloves garlic
- 3 tablespoons Sambal bajak (recipe page 23)
- salt, pepper
- 1 tablespoon groundnut oil

Preparation
Dice the large aubergines. Cut the small aubergines in half and cover all of them with salt. Chop up the chicken or shrimps. Peel the garlic and chop finely. Peel the shallots and cut into small cubes. Heat the oil in a pan. Fry the garlic and shallots until transparent. Add the aubergines and fry briefly, stirring continuously, then add the chopped chicken or shrimps. Cook, stirring continuously and after about 3 minutes, stir in the sambal little by little. Finally, season with salt and pepper.

Tip: If this dish is too fiery for some tastes, replace the sambal with fresh, peeled, chopped tomatoes. If shrimps are used, Kerupuk udang (crisp beef skin) is a perfect accompaniment. Otherwise, serve rice with it. The dish can also be served as a vegetable dish with meat dishes, fish or chicken.

Sayur lodèh waluh

Quantities for 4–6 people:
500 g/18 oz various vegetables, for instance green or yellow beans, carrots, bamboo shoots, sweetcorn, white cabbage, paprika, aubergine, squash
100 g/3½ oz tofu (bean curd)

Vegetable and coconut stew

Preparation
Peel the vegetables if necessary, then cut into cubes or sticks. Cut up the tofu and tempe in the same way. Peel the shallots and garlic and pound together with

coriander, cumin and trasi. Wash the chillies and cut into pieces of 1 cm/⅜ in. Peel and crush the galangal root.

Add the coconut milk (thin) and bring to the boil with all the spices, then add the vegetables, tofu and tempe (these may also be deep fried in advance). Simmer fro 12–15 minutes. Serve with rice.

> Tip: Sayur lodèh is delicious served with kerupuk and sambal trasi (recipe page 29). Naturally, it is also always served with rice.

100 g/3½ oz tempe
5 shallots
3 cloves garlic
1 teaspoon coriander
½ teaspoon cumin
1 teaspoon trasi (shrimp paste)
1 red and 1 green chillies
2–3 kaffir lime leaves
1 piece galangal root, about 2.5 cm/1 in long
2 salam leaves (or bay leaves)
1 litre/1¾ pints (4½ cups) coconut milk

Lotèk

Salad with peanut and potato dressing

A traditional vegetable dish from West Java.

Preparation

Wash and prepare the vegetables, peel and cut into small pieces and blanch briefly apart from the cucumber and lettuce. Cut the tofu into cubes and fry or, better still, deep fry. Wash the lettuce and pull it apart. Stir the blanched vegetables together with the deep-fried tofu, cucumber pieces and salad.

Grind the peanuts, chillies, palm sugar and tamarind together with the trasi and kencur. Stir in the potato, mashing it so that it amalgamates with the rest of the ingredients. Add the lemon juice and a little water to thin the mixture slightly. Pour this thick, sour dressing over the blanched vegetables. Served with kerupuk or emping, it makes an ideal light meal. But accompanied by ketupat (recipe page 108), it becomes a meal in its own right.

Quantities for 4 people:
Various vegetables, for instance:
  75 g/3 oz kangkung (water spinach) (or watercress or lamb's lettuce (75 g), 1 manisah (or kohlrabi), 1 bunch pak choi (or Swiss chard), 1 cabbage
1 small head lettuce
½ cucumber
150 g/5 oz tofu (bean curd)

For the dressing:
100 g/3½ oz (1 cup) roasted, unsalted peanuts
2–3 chillies or 1 red chilli (medium hot)
1 tablespoon palm sugar
1 teaspoon tamarind mousse or concentrate
1 teaspoon trasi (shrimp paste)
½ teaspoon kencur
juice of 1 lemon
1 large cooked potato
salt, water

Kencur

Gado gado Atim

Mixed vegetables with peanut sauce

Quantities for 3–4 people:
100 g/3½ oz green beans
100 g/3½ oz soya bean sprouts
¼ small white cabbage
½ cucumber
½ small head lettuce
2 boiled potatoes
100 g/3½ oz tofu (bean curd)
100 g/3½ oz tempe
1 hard-boiled (hard-cooked) egg
1 handful roast onions
kerupuk
emping (crisp pancakes)

For the sauce:
250 g/9 oz (2½ cups) unsalted, dry-roasted peanuts
3 cloves garlic
1 cooked sweet potato
1 teaspoon Sambal ulek (or more to taste, recipe page 23)
2–3 tablespoons palm sugar (or brown sugar)
200 ml/7 fl oz (⅞ cup) coconut milk
coconut oil
vinegar
salt

As anyone who has been to Indonesia or an Indonesian restaurant will know, gado gado is a traditional Indonesian dish. This recipe is called Gado gado Atim after a man who used to carry his food basket through the streets of the Javanese hill city of Malang every day just before midday. Often he would stop near the school buildings of Jl Panderman where he eventually came to know by name all the pupils who used to sneak out of school to go and eat some of his delicious gado gado. He even gave them credit when they had no money. Atim was extremely popular and he was soon able to swap his basket for a food cart.

Preparation

Wash the vegetables. Cut the white cabbage into strips and the cucumbers into sticks and blanch. Dice the boiled potatoes. Cut the tempe and tofu into cubes and deep fry.

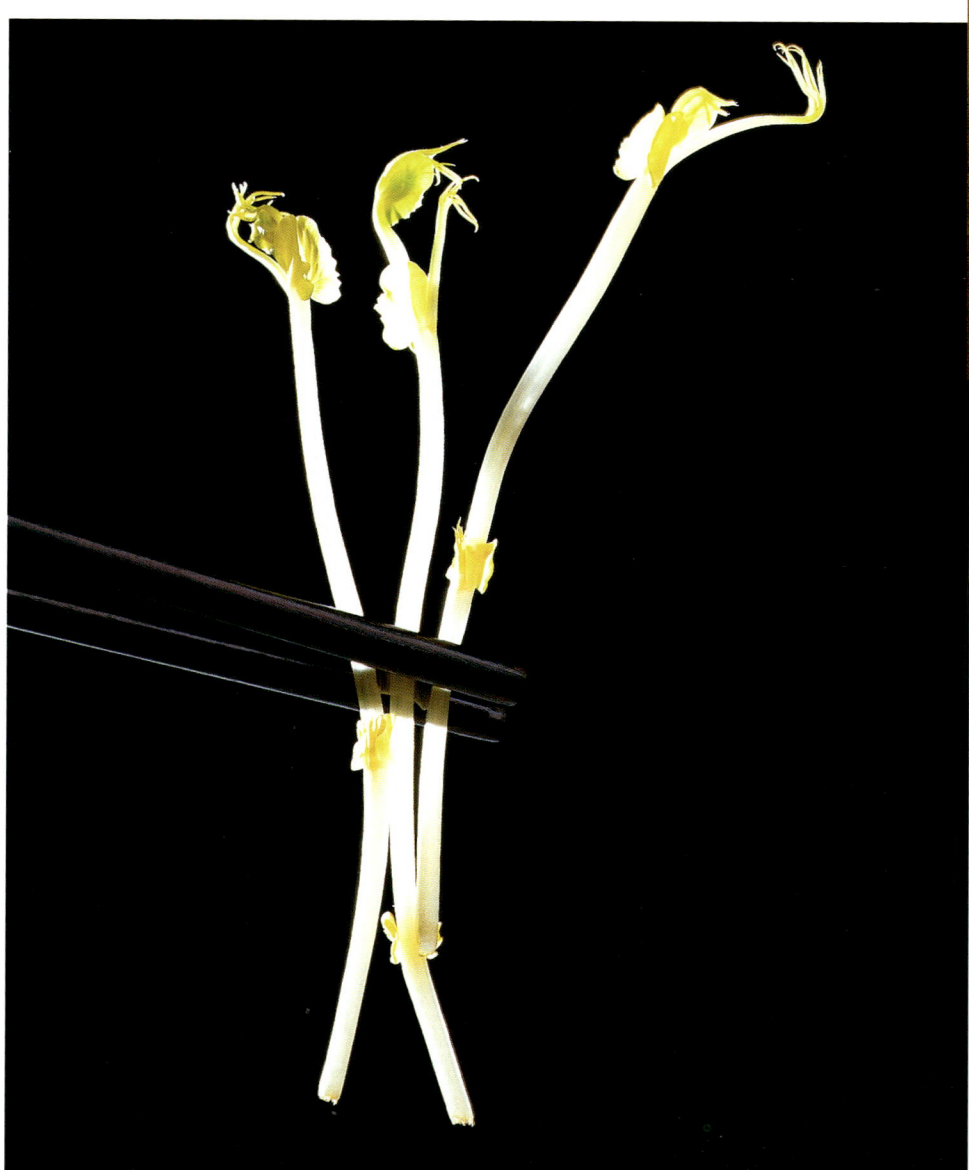

Crunchy crackers, crisps and sticks: different types of kerupuk and emping.

To make the sauce, puree the peanuts and garlic with the boiled and peeled sweet potatoes in a blender together with sambal and sugar. Then fry the paste in coconut oil. Add the coconut milk little by little, stirring continuously and bringing it slowly to the boil until the mixture no longer sticks to the bottom. If necessary, dilute the sauce with a little water. Season with salt and vinegar so that the sauce is both sweet and sour.

Arrange the vegetables and tofu on a dish. Cut the hard-boiled egg into four quarters or into slices and place around the vegetable and tofu. Pour the sauce on top and garnish with the fried onions, kerupuk and emping.

This dish can be served on its own or with rice or Lontong (recipe page 108).

Sambal goreng tomat

Tomatoes in sambal-goreng sauce

Quantities for 4–6 people, provided the dish is accompanied by filling side dishes
- 5 firm tomatoes
- 5 shallots
- 3 cloves garlic
- 2 red chillies
- 1 piece galangal root, about 5 cm/2 in long
- ½ teaspoon trasi (shrimp paste)
- 3 salam leaves (or bay leaves)
- 2 cups coconut milk
- 2 tablespoons coconut oil

Preparation

Cut the tomatoes in half. Peel the shallots and garlic and chop finely. Cut the red chillies diagonally into thin strips. Peel the galangal roots and crush. Heat the coconut oil, add the chopped shallot and garlic and fry, then add remaining ingredients except for the coconut milk and continue frying. Next add the coconut milk and bring to the boil. It is delicious served with dishes based on tofu (bean curd) and tempe, such as Gimbal mawut (recipe page 86).

Tip: This dish can also be prepared with fish fillet, mussels or shrimps, or with different vegetables.

VEGETABLE AND TOFU DISHES | 97

Sayur kare

Vegetable curry

Preparation
Wash the vegetables thoroughly, peel if necessary and cut up or chop the vegetables as appropriate: carrots into slices, kohlrabi into sticks, and so on.

Heat the vegetable stock and add the kaffir lime leaves, lemon grass, cardamom (crush the pods), cinnamon and cloves. Meanwhile, grind the ingredients for the spicy paste and fry in oil. Add the fried spicy paste to the hot vegetable stock and add the vegetables little by little. Continue simmering for a few more minutes. Finally, stir in the coconut milk. Heat the mixture again until it is hot enough.

Quantities for 4–6 people:
Selection of vegetables according to taste and availability, such as:
2 carrots
1 kohlrabi
100 g/3½ oz green beans
100 g/3½ oz bamboo sprouts
50 g/2 oz sweetcorn
1 red pepper
¼ cauliflower
1 small cabbage
2 potatoes

Other ingredients
500 ml/17 fl oz (2¼ cups) vegetable stock (broth)
2 kaffir lime leaves
1 stem lemon grass
1 cardamom pod
1 cinnamon stick
1–2 cloves
400 ml/14 fl oz (1¾ cups) coconut milk (canned)

For the spicy paste:
7 shallots
3 cloves garlic
5 kemiri nuts (or macadamia nuts)
1 teaspoon ground coriander
1 teaspoon ground turmeric
1 teaspoon tamarind mousse
2 slices fresh ginger root
pinch each of cumin, nutmeg, salt and pepper
2 tablespoons oil for frying

Quantities for 4 people:
½ cucumber
½ pineapple
1–2 sharp apples
1–2 carambola (star fruit)
½ jicama
1 kohlrabi or ⅓ radish
½ jeruk bali (pomelo)

For the sauce
2–3 tablespoons palm sugar
1–2 tablespoons tamarind mousse
2–3 chillies
1 teaspoon Sambal ulek (recipe page 23) (optional)
1 teaspoon trasi (shrimp paste)

Rujak manis

Fruit and vegetable salad with palm sugar dressing

Preparation
Melt the palm sugar and add a little water if necessary. Leave to cool. Chop the chillies finely and stir into the palm sugar together with the other ingredients for the sauce.

Peel the fruit and vegetables if necessary and cut into bite-sized pieces, perhaps in different shapes. Put in a bowl and pour over the sauce.

VEGETABLE AND TOFU DISHES | 99

Asparagus tumis kepiting

Wild asparagus with crabmeat

This dish is ideal as a side salad or starter.

Preparation
Cut off the woody bottom part of the asparagus and peel the lower part lightly if necessary. Wash the asparagus. Peel the garlic and cut into thin slices. Steam the crab meat. Heat the oil over medium heat, add the garlic and fry until golden brown. Add the asparagus and stir well. Cook briefly – the vegetable should be "al dente". Arrange on a dish with the steamed crab. Season with salt and pepper.

    This salad is also delicious as topping on an omelette.

Quantities for 4 people:
2 bunches wild asparagus
500 g/18 oz crabmeat
2 cloves garlic
2 tablespoons macadamia nut oil
salt, pepper

Rice and noodle dishes

Rice dishes – Nasi

In Indonesia the range of dishes based on rice – *nasi* – is very wide and varied. There are also many types of rice such as red rice, *beras merah*, a wild rice. Rice is served boiled, steamed or fried as a side dish, as in the well-known Nasi goreng; it is also made into rice cakes. On certain festive days such as those of *Selamatan*, the great ritual banquet, *ketupat* (rice parcels) are very popular. In Bali, *sesajen*, beautiful pouches made from plaited palm leaves in which rice is cooked are presented to the gods as offerings. Rice is also used to make puddings such as Beras ketan hitam, black sticky rice.

Rice is either cooked in the normal way, or it may first be par-boiled, then put in a sieve suspended in a saucepan filled with water in which it is steamed until it is cooked. This method is very popular and is similar to the traditional method that uses a *dandang*, a special metal steamer, or a *dukasan*, a bamboo sieve. As a rule of thumb, two cups of rice need three and a half cups of liquid.

> "Yellow rice pressed into a conical shape, Nasi tumpeng, is used as the centrepiece of traditional banquets."

Nasi liwet
Rice cooked in a clay pot

This dish is traditionally cooked in a clay pot, covered with a banana leaf that will give its distinctive aroma to the rice.

Preparation
Wash the rice thoroughly and put it in a saucepan of cold water. The rice should be covered with water to a depth as thick as a finger. Cover and bring to the boil. As soon as the water has been absorbed by the rice, stir it briefly and reduce the heat to the lowest flame possible. Keep covered and continue cooking for another 10–15 minutes.

Quantities for 4 people:
500 g/18 oz rice
about 750 ml/1¼ pints (3½ cups) cold water

White rice may also be served separately depending on the dish or the occasion.

Nasi kuning

Yellow rice

Quantities for 4 people:
300 g/10 oz perfumed or other long grain rice
100 g/3½ oz sticky rice
500 ml/17 fl oz (2¼ cups) coconut milk
1 stem lemon grass
3 kaffir lime leaves
juice of ½ lemon
1 Pandanusblatt
1 teaspoon turmeric
salt

A dish of yellow rice is often the focal point of banquets in Java. It is called Nasi tumpeng when it arranged in a cone-shaped mound and accompanied by various mouthwatering dishes (see illustration page 100).

Preparation
First thoroughly wash the sticky rice and soak in water for 1–2 hours. This is necessary because the cooking times of the two kinds of rice is not the same. Wash the other rice thoroughly, put both in a saucepan and mix well. Stir together the other ingredients to make a stock and pour over the rice so that it is covered with about 12 mm/½ in of liquid. Bring to the boil over medium heat and cook without a lid until all the water has been absorbed and there are no longer any bubbles between the grains of rice. Now reduce the heat to the lowest possible flame and cover. Continue cooking over a low flame while carefully loosening the rice with a fork.

To follow the traditional cooking method, the rice is steamed in a bamboo steamer or in steamer basket placed over boiling water for 15–20 minutes.

Dishes served at a Selamatan

The traditional dishes served at a Selamatan include roast chicken, omelette, eggs and roast onions (see illustration page 100), which combine beautifully with Nasi kuning or Nasi kabuli. The range of dishes may also include other dishes such as Urap urap (recipe page 87) and Ikan bumbu Bali (recipe page 72). The dishes offered depend not only on the host's financial prosperity but also on the occasion of the invitation. Very often mutton is slaughtered and roasted on a spit, and the guests will often go home with a small basket filled with left-over mutton. The traditional *wayang kulit*, Indonesian shadow theatre, has survived in many villages and the occasion consists involves watching, praying and eating together. The food is eaten with the fingers of the right hand from a banana leaf that serves as plate.

Nasi kabuli

"Rice of fulfilment"

A spicier version of Nasi kuning is Nasi kabuli – rice for the fulfilment of wishes. The word *kabul* is derived from *terkabul*, meaning "fulfilment". This rice-based dish is often served at Selamatans, banquets, instead of the normal rice.

Preparation

Wash the sticky rice and soak for 1–2 hours. Cook the ingredients for spicy stock in water for about 20 minutes. Wash the normal rice and mix with the sticky rice. Stir together to coconut milk, the spicy stock (having first removed the spices), the other spices and add to the rice. Cook in the same way as Nasi kuning (opposite).

Quantities for 4 people:
300 g perfumed or other long grain rice
100 g/3½ oz sticky rice
400 ml/14 fl oz (1¾ cups) coconut milk
1 stem lemon grass
3 kaffir lime leaves
juice of ½ lemon
1 pandanus leaf
1 teaspoon turmeric
salt

For the spicy stock:
150 ml/5 fl oz (⅝ cup) water
½ teaspoon ground coriander
¼ teaspoon ground cumin
1 cinnamon stick
1 piece galangal root, 2 cm/¾ in long
1 stem lemon grass
3 pandanus leaves
1 salam leaf (or bay leaf)
2 cloves
2 cardamom pod or 1 teaspoon ground cardamom
pinch of nutmeg
salt

Nasi uduk

Rice in coconut milk

This cooking method originates from West Java (see illustration opposite).

Quantities for 4 people:
500 g/18 oz long grain rice
about 750 ml/1¼ pints (3½ cups) coconut milk
2 pandanus leaves
salt

Preparation
Wash the rice thoroughly and bring to the boil in a saucepan together with the coconut milk and pandanus leaves, seasoned to taste with salt. Once boiling, reduce the heat until the liquid has been absorbed, which will take about 10 minutes. Be careful that the rice does not burn. Then cook for another 15-20 minutes in a steamer as described for Nasi liwet (recipe page 101).

This may be served for instance with Ayam goreng ijo (recipe page 51), peanuts and strips of omelette.

Nasi ayam santen

Rice with chicken in coconut milk

Quantities for 4–5 people:
1 chicken 1–1.2 kg/2¼–2½ lb
about 750 ml/1¼ pints (3½ cups) coconut milk
500 g/18 oz long grain rice
1 cinnamon stick
white pepper
salt

Preparation
Clean the chicken and cut into eight or ten pieces. Put in a saucepan with the coconut milk. Season with salt and pepper and cook for about 20 minutes until it is partially cooked. Put to one side.

Wash the rice thoroughly and place in a saucepan. Put the partially cooked chicken in the middle of the rice. Add the sticks of cinnamon and pour the coconut stock on top. Add some water if necessary: the rice should be covered with about 12 mm/½ in of liquid. Bring to the boil, reduce the heat, then cook the rice and chicken together for a further 15 minutes.

This dish is served with Sambal manis (recipe page 28).

Tip: If a more granular rice is preferred, separate it gently with a fork towards the end of the cooking period.

Quantities for 4 people:
- 4 cups cooked rice
- 2 eggs
- Meat to taste, and shrimps, or a mixture of several kinds of meat such as chicken and pork
- 5 shallots
- 2 cloves garlic
- 5 red chillies
- 1 tomato
- 1 teaspoon trasi (shrimp paste)
- 1 tablespoon kecap manis (sweet soy sauce)
- salt, pepper
- 2 tablespoons vegetable oil

Nasi goreng

Fried rice

Preparation

Peel the shallots and garlic. Wash the chillies (to make the dish less hot, remove the seeds). Wash the tomatoes and cut into pieces. Grind these ingredients together with the trasi, salt and pepper and stir well. Then fry this spicy mixture in the oil. Briefly scramble the eggs in another pan. Add the scrambled egg to the spicy mixture together with the pieces of meat, shrimps and kecap manis. Add the rice, stir well and continue frying while stirring continuously.

Nasi goreng is delicious served with fried egg or omelette, and also sate, salad and kerupuk. The kind and number of dishes depends on whether it is served at breakfast, midday or evening.

Ketan

Steamed sticky rice

Preparation

Soak the sticky rice in plenty of water for about 2 hours. Place the rice in the water in which it has soaked and bring to the boil. Cook for 10 minutes. Then place the rice in a sieve in a bamboo or ordinary steamer, add the pandanus leaf and steam for about another 15 minutes. Add the coconut milk to the rice little by little and stir well. Season with salt and pepper. When the sticky rice is slightly transparent, it is ready. Sprinkle with abon and grated coconut before serving.

Quantities for 4 people:
500 g/18 oz (2 cups) sticky rice
500 ml/17 fl oz (2¼ cups) coconut milk
pinch of salt
1 pandanus leaf
1 cup desiccated (shredded) coconut
1 cup abon

Lontong and ketupat

Lontong and ketupat are dishes in which the rice is cooked in leaves (lontong). Ketupat is more elaborate version because the palm leaves are plaited beforehand. On days preceding Muslim festivals such as Idul Fitri, women and children sit for hours plaiting palm leaves.

Lontong or ketupat are served with dishes such as sambal goreng manisah, sayur karé or simply with sate or soto (soup). At breakfast lontong is often served with gado gado or the very similar lontong pecel. Here is the recipe for Lontong cap goh meh èbès.

Lontong cap goh meh èbès

Rice in a banana leaf

There is a particular story behind this dish. Originally it was a festival dish, prepared by expatriate Chinese families (Huaqiao) in Indonesia, which took place 15 days after Imlek, the Chinese New Year. *Cap* means "ten" and *goh* means "five" in southern Chinese Fujian dialect. In fact, this dish does not exist in Chinese cuisine but it is a classic example of a combination of the various cultures in Asia. The preparation of 15 different dishes served by maids at the banquet might take two days to complete. In addition, the family altar was also decorated and the ancestors were brought bowls of food.

Nowadays, many food stalls and restaurants offer these banquet dishes as a

speciality without being aware of their tradition. Most dishes served with lontong are prepared with coconut. For many, Lontong cap goh meh èbès has very nostalgic connotations. It is a homage to all mothers who left Indonesia to build a new life abroad but bringing with them their traditions and cultural and culinary heritage in order to pass them on to their descendants – from New York to Cologne, from Melbourne to Amsterdam.

Here is the recipe for Lontong.

Preparation
Wash the rice thoroughly and drain. Soak the banana leaves in water to soften them and fold them into tubes 5–7 cm/2–3 in in diameter and 10–20 cm/4–8 in long (depending on the size of the leaf and the pan available). Seal one end with a bamboo stick or toothpick. Fill the tube one-third full with the washed rice and close the open end. Next cook the these rice-filled tubes for 2–3 hours in plenty of water. Add water now and again to make sure that the tubes are always covered so that the rice cooks evenly. At the end of the cooking time, remove the lontong from the water and leave them to cool down. Unroll each one and carefully cut into slices 1–2 cm/⅜–¾ in thick.

If banana leaves are not available, buy three bags of boil-in-the-bag rice. Fold over the empty part of each bag and form the rice into a cylindrical shape so that the "rice cake" has the same shape as a real lontong. Secure by sewing or pinning together. Then follow the same cooking process as described above.

The meal might be completed with the following dishes: Vegetable curry, Chicken in rujak sauce, Quails' eggs in coconut cream, Small crabs in bamboo and coconut sauce, Saddle of rabbit with lily flowers and green tea leaves, Cutlet in date and mushroom sauce, Crabs or shrimps in sambal goreng, Red snapper in red sauce, Yellow-coloured, Abon and Dèndèng relishes, Spicy-sweet spicy soya bean powder, Serundeng and Fried tempe sticks.

Quantities for 4 people:
500 g/18 oz rice
banana leaves for wrapping

"Delicious lontong are excellent with sate, such as Rayuan pulau kelapa (recipe page 60) or a simple Sate ayam"

Noodle dishes

As with rice there are many kinds of noodles, made from all kinds of ingredients. Rice noodles, *bihun*, are particularly popular in West Java. Noodles are a major ingredient in Ketroprak, a dish consisting of vegetables, tofu (bean curd), emping, kerupuk and peanut-soy sauce. Another popular dish is Bihun goreng, fried noodles with meat, prawns and vegetables including cabbage, soya bean (soybean) sprouts and pak choi. Nyonya cuisine also includes Laksa, yellow chicken curry on a bed of rice noodles with soya bean sprouts and other side dishes. Last but not least there is the soup *bihun kuah*, widely exported in cans or deep-frozen. *Kuetai*, wide noodles, also made from rice, are often fried with other ingredients. Besides rice noodles, there are also the transparent noodles that are an integral part of the island's cuisine. Made from mung bean flour, they are a major ingredients of the chicken soup Soto ayam, for instance.

Egg noodles, *mie telor*, come in various shapes: thin or wide, crinkled or smooth. To make Mie jawa, fresh, slightly thicker egg noodles are used.

Java and Bali have given rise to a variety of egg noodle dishes and, typically of Indonesia, there are many food stalls and a number of restaurants specializing in one or the other. Mie kerak is undoubtedly the national dish of West Java where it is sold everywhere on the street. Mie godok, a noodle soup is found throughout West and East Java as well as in Bali. Fried Mie goreng, on the other hand, is only found in Jakarta. Finally, the pastry made from it is used a case for Lumpia (spring rolls) and Pangsit parcels.

Mie jawa

Quantities for 4 people:
500–600 g fresh egg noodles
250 g/9 oz cooked chicken or beef
1 piece galangal root,
 about 2 cm/¾ in long
2 cloves garlic
2 chillies
5 leeks
1 handful white cabbage
1 handful soya bean (soybean)
 sprouts
1½ tablespoons kecap manis (sweet
 soy sauce)
1 teaspoon trasi (shrimp paste)
salt
2 tablespoons coconut oil for frying
some chicken stock (broth) or water
1 bunch celery leaves to garnish
1 handful fried onions

Fried noodles with meat and vegetables

Preparation
Peel and crush the galangal root. Peel the garlic and cut into thin slices. Cut the chillies into thin strips. Also cut the cooked chicken or beef in strips. Wash and prepare the leeks and cut into diagonal slices. Cut the cabbage into strips and wash. Wash the soya bean sprouts and celery leaves and chop finely.

Heat the coconut oil in a large, deep pan (preferably a wok) and fry the garlic until brown. Then add the meat, the vegetables apart from the celery leaves and the spices. Add a little liquid (water or chicken stock) and stir in the noodles. Heat up this mixture, sprinkle with celery and fried onions and serve.

Mie babah

Noodles with meat and mushroom ragout

Unusually for Indonesia, this dish may be eaten with chopsticks, a fact that reflects the Chinese influence. In this region food is traditionally eaten with the fingers of the right hand or with a fork and spoon; the spoon plays the part of the fork in the west, being held in the right hand to carry the food to the mouth.

Quantities for 4 people:
500 g/18 oz thin egg noodles
250 g/9 oz cabbage, or alternatively
 spinach
salt
pepper
3–5 drops sesame oil
2 tablespoons soy sauce

Preparation
Cook the noodles as usual in boiling salted water, drain and add the spices and stir. Blanch the vegetables and add to the noodles. Peel the garlic, cut into slices and fry in peanut oil. Cut the meat into small cubes and add to the garlic in the pan. Fry briskly. Then add the mushrooms, ebi and oyster sauce as well as the spring onions, cut into rings. Pour over the stock. Reserve some spring onions for the garnish. Season with pepper and soy sauce.

Put the noodles in a large bowl and pour the ragout on top. Garnish with the remaining spring onions.

This is served with the dried radish preserve tong cai, chilli preserve and mixed pickles.

For the ragout:
2 pork cutlets or chicken breast fillets
2 cloves garlic
1 handful mushrooms
1 handful ebi (dried shrimps) or fresh shrimps
2–3 tablespoons oyster sauce
1 bunch spring onions (scallions)
½ cup chicken stock (broth)
1 tablespoon kecap manis (sweet soy sauce)
pepper
2 tablespoons groundnut oil

Lumpia basah

Quantities for 20–25 pieces
For the cases:
250 g/9 oz wheat flour
250 ml/8 fl oz (1 cup) water
2 eggs
salt
1 tablespoon groundnut oil

For the stuffing:
5 shallots
2 cloves garlic
1 small bunch celery leaves
1 small bunch spring onions (scallions)
1 cup soya bean (soybean) sprouts
1 cup finely chopped meat (chicken or pork)
½ cup small shrimps, shelled, or crabmeat
½ cup bamboo shoots
1 tablespoon soy sauce
1 tablespoon kecap manis (sweet soy sauce)
2 tablespoons oil to sauté

Spring rolls

Preparation

First make the wafer-thin pastry used to wrap the stuffing. Beat the eggs until foamy, add salt and stir in the flour little by little. Add the water also a little at a time and briskly whisk this very thin batter (similar to pancake batter). Heat a pan and coat with a little oil. Fry the batter in very thin layers.

To make the stuffing, peel the shallots and garlic and chop both finely. Wash the celery leaves and cut into fine strips. Wash and trim the spring onions and cut into thin rings. Cut the bamboo into thin strips. Wash the soya bean sprouts.

Next fry the garlic and shallots, then add the meat, shrimp or crabmeat and bamboo shoots. Add the spices together with the spring leek onions cut into rings and the chopped-up celery leaves. Finally stir in the soya bean sprouts and sauté for about 5 minutes.

Put 2–3 tablespoons of the stuffing on a each pancake, then fold over on three sides and roll. Serve the spring rolls with Sambal taoco (recipe page 24).

If you want to deep fry the lumpia, frozen spring roll pastry is recommended (it comes in several sizes, large and small squares). The filling is the same as for Lumpia basah. Alternatively other vegetables can be used, such as carrots cut into sticks or white cabbage, cut into strips. Fish and seafood can also be used.

Ready-made dough gives the opportunity to allow the imagination free rein. Place a spoonful of filling in the middle of a square of pastry, gather it together like a pouch and secure with a some chives. Try making pouches or parcels filled with finely diced tuna fish or with various kinds of seafood (prawns, cuttlefish or mussels are perfect for this). Add leeks, garlic, ginger, salt and pepper as well as an egg and a little flour to the filling so that it holds it together and becomes more solid. The "parcels" can then be fried or deep-fried in oil.

"Use all your imagination and creativity in making these little parcels"

Telaga warna

Transparent noodles with mixed vegetables, chicken and fish balls

Quantities for 4 people:
- about 250 g/9 oz mung bean noodles
- ½ cup dried mu'erh mushrooms
- ½ cup dried lily flower buds
- ½ cup sugar peas
- ½ cup thinly sliced chopped carrots
- ½–1 leak
- 1 whole cooked chicken breast fillets
- 2 cloves garlic
- ½ cup rice straw mushrooms (preserved)
- ½ cup asparagus tips
- 500 ml/17 fl oz (2¼ cups) chicken stock (broth)
- 50 ml/1½ fl oz (3 tablespoons) rice wine
- pinch of sugar
- 1 tablespoon tapioca flour
- oil

For the fish balls:
- 1 cup prawns, or about 250 g/9 oz fillet of fish,
- 1 egg
- salt
- pepper

Preparation

Soak the lily flowers, transparent noodles and mu'erh-mushrooms separately (the transparent noodles should be soaked in hot water). Blanch the sugar peas and pieces of carrots. Cut the chicken breasts into wafer-thin slices.

For the fish balls, finely chop the prawns or fish, season with salt and pepper and stir in the egg. Reserve 2 tablespoons forcemeat and form the rest into little balls. Cook in boiling water. Simmer until they rise to the surface of the water – which means they are ready. Take out of the water.

Peel the cloves of garlic and cut into thin slices. Heat 1 tablespoon of oil in a wok or deep saucepan and fry the garlic until golden brown. Briefly stir-fry the other ingredients (vegetables, chicken and fish balls) in the wok or pan. Add the chicken stock and heat up again. Season with a dash of rice wine and season. Add the 2 tablespoons of reserved forcemeat. Stir a little water into the tapioca flour and add to the ingredients in the wok, stir and allow to thicken. Pour over the drained transparent noodles.

Tip: Instead of transparent noodles, wide egg noodles or rice noodles may be used.

Noodles are often used in soup.

Pangsit goreng

Pastry parcels stuffed with meat

Preparation
Mix together the wheat flour and tapioca flour with the eggs, oil or fat and knead, adding water little by little, until a smooth dough that no longer sticks to the hands is formed. Then dust the dough with tapioca flour and roll it out as thinly as possible. Cut into squares 10 x 10 cm/4 x 4in.

Wash the ingredients for the filling and the chives and chop up. Mix well. Place 1–2 tablespoons of this filling in the middle of each square of dough. Fold the corners of the squares on top of each other so as to make a triangle. Make a dent lengthways in the middle of the triangle to create a kind of butterfly shape. Deep-fry in plenty of oil.

These "pastry parcels" make ideal starters. They are delicious served with Sambal cuka (recipe page 29) or Sambal bawang pulith (recipe page 31).

Quantities for 6–10 people, about 30 parcels

For the pastry:
250 g/9 oz 1 cup wheat flour
2 tablespoons tapioca flour
2 eggs
1 tablespoon pork fat or oil
salt
about 1 cup water
1 tablespoon tapioca flour for dusting

For the stuffing:
about 500 g/18 oz pork or chicken, mixed with minced shrimp
salt
pepper
1 tablespoon fish sauce
1 bunch chives
oil for frying

Pangsit kuah

Pastry parcels cooked in stock

Pangsit are ideal for adding to soup. The method used to make the dough, forcemeat and parcels is exactly the same as that for Pangsit goreng above. But instead of deep frying the pastry parcels, they are cooked for a few minutes in boiling water until they rise to the surface, which means that they are ready. The pangsit are then added to clear chicken soup seasoned with salt and pepper. The soup is completed by the addition of chives, fried onions and a few vegetables, such as spinach, cauliflower, and pak choi.

Desserts and puddings

There are no desserts and puddings in the European sense in Indonesian cuisine. Sweetmeats or puddings can be eaten throughout the day. Puddings and cakes made from rice, in particular sticky rice, are very popular. Mung beans, palm sugar, pandanus leaves and coconut give Indonesian puddings their distinctive flavour. There is sago and coconut pudding, black sticky rice in coconut milk dessert and puddings made with agar and coconut milk or cows' milk, often served with fruit. There are also many cakes and torte recipes of Dutch origin, ranging from spiced cake to buttercream torte.

Onde nenas

Sesame balls stuffed with pineapple

Preparation

For the filling: first peel the fresh pineapple and cut into small pieces. Add sugar and simmer, stirring continuously, until a jam-like consistency is reached. (If tinned pineapple is used, add less sugar because it has already been sweetened.) The coconut alternative is made by simply stirring sugar into the grated coconut.

Add the egg, sugar, salt and water to the sticky rice and rice flour and mix to obtain a smooth but fairly firm mass. Make small balls 5–7 cm/2–3 in in diameter with this mixture. Make a hollow in the centre of each one and fill with pineapple or grated coconut. Close up the hollow again. Coat in sesame seeds. Heat the oil and deep fry the sesame balls over medium heat until golden brown.

Quantities for 10–12 pieces
2 cups sticky rice
1 tablespoon rice flour
1 egg
2 teaspoons sugar
pinch of salt
1–2 cups tepid water
1 cup sesame seeds
oil for frying

For the stuffing:
1 cup fresh pineapple and ½ cup sugar
or 1 cup desiccated (shredded) coconut and ½ cup sugar

Es apokat moka

Avocado and coffee parfait

Preparation

Peel the avocado and remove the stone. Cut into small cubes and sprinkle with lime juice.

Bring the milk, cream and coconut milk to the boil and reduce a little. Beat the egg yolk until foamy, take the milk from the heat and carefully fold in the egg yolk. Leave to cool.

Stir the instant coffee into the sugar syrup. Next place the diced avocado in a metal mould and pour the milk mixture on top. Freeze for 3–4 hours in a 3-star freezer compartment. Cut into slices before serving and sprinkle with coffee liqueur if desired.

Quantities for 4–6 people:
1 large, ripe avocado
juice of ½–1 lime
150 ml/5 fl oz (5/8 cup) cream
50 ml/1½ fl oz (3 tablespoons) milk
50 ml/1½ fl oz (3 tablespoons) coconut milk
1 egg yokk
100 ml/3½ fl oz (½ cup) thin sugar syrup
1 tablespoon instant coffee
coffee liqueur to taste

Putu gedang

Steamed cooking bananas

Quantities for 2 people:
1 ripe cooking banana
about 1 cup desiccated (shredded) coconut
1 tablespoon vanilla sugar

Preparation
Steam the cooking bananas in their skins until they are tender inside. Remove from the skin and cut into not thin slices. Sprinkle with grated coconut and vanilla sugar and serve warm.

Kue lumpur

Small coconut cakes

These pastries are examples of the kind of food that many families make early in the morning (between three and seven o'clock in the morning) and sell from home to make extra money. Neighbours come by at about 6.30 a.m. and buy the little cakes. Any left over are taken to the market later.

Many families cook food including little cakes such as these Kue lumpur as an extra source of income.

Preparation

Beat the egg and sugar until foamy. Fold the coconut milk, flour and pulp very gently into the beaten egg and sugar and stir carefully to obtain a smooth mixture. The dough is fried in a special cast iron pan with separate hollows. Heat the pan and grease it with margarine. Put the dough in the hollows in the pan and decorate each little cake with a raisin. The little cakes can also be baked in small moulds in the oven for about 15 minutes at a temperature of 180°C (350°F), Gas mark 4.

Quantities for about 20 cakes:
5 eggs
125 ml/4 fl oz (½ cup) sugar
250 g/9 oz wheat flour
1 vanilla pod
1.25 litres/2¼ pints (5½ cups) coconut milk
Currants to garnish

Serabi itam manis

Quantities for 8–10 cakes:

For the serabi:
1 cup wheat flour
1 teaspoon dried yeast
1 egg
375 ml/12 fl oz (1½ cups) coconut milk
1 teaspoon icing (confectioners') sugar
pinch of salt

For the hitam manis:
1 cup black sticky rice
1.25 litres/2¼ pints (5½ cups) water
1 pandanus leaf
sugar to taste

500 ml/17 fl oz (2¼ cups) coconut cream
1 pandanus leaf
pinch of salt

Small cakes with black sticky rice and coconut cream

Preparation
Heat the coconut milk and stir the yeast, flour and egg into it. The mixture should have a consistency similar to pancake batter. Leave to stand for 30 minutes. Heat a wok or small saucepan and brush with a little oil. Put a small ladle of dough in the wok or in each hollow of the cast-iron pan (about 1 cm/⅜ in deep), cover and fry for 3–5 minutes until ready.

Carefully wash the black sticky rice for the hitam manis. Add the pandanus leaf and sugar to the water and bring to the boil. Then simmer for about 25 minutes over low to medium heat (as if cooking porridge).

In a separate pan, heat up the coconut cream with a pinch of salt and another pandanus leaf.

Arrange each warm, freshly made serabi on a plate with two or three tablespoons of sticky rice. Then pour three tablespoons of coconut cream on top.

Drinks

The range of hot and cold drinks in Indonesia is enormous. Indonesians are very partial to sweet jasmine or Malabar tea (black tea), hot or cold . In Indonesia coffee can become a real energy-boosting drink made with egg, honey and spices such as ginger or beras kencur, a popular way to start a long day of hard physical labour.

Cold drinks include herbal mixtures known as *jamu*, which may be sweet, sour or bitter, and syrups such as rose, tamarind or fruit syrup diluted with coconut milk or water and ice. Indonesians are also very fond of iced fruit drinks, produced by blending various fruits with ice cubes in a mixer, known as the *es juice*. An example is *es apokat*, avocado with coffee extract, sugar, sweetened milk and ice cubes, puréed in the mixer. Mango with ice cubes and a little lemon juice is prepared in the same way and produces a kind of sorbet-like drink. Another such drink is jackfruit, puréed with coconut milk, durian, sugar syrup and ice cubes. There is also palm juice but the latter ferments rather quickly. Palm wine is made, and there is also the very alcoholic palm schnapps (arrak).

Beer is also brewed in Indonesia, mostly from rice.

Festivals in Bali and Java

It would be impossible to imagine Indonesia without its colourful festivals and magnificent ceremonies. In Indonesia – and more especially in Bali – religious and traditional life is punctuated by a series of festivals and ceremonies marking every important event.

In Java, life is dominated by Muslim festivals – although here too there are festivals dating back to pre-Islamic times. In Bali, however, most festivals are celebrations of the Hindu Dharma religion or of even older popular beliefs that survived the arrival of Islam on the "island of the gods".

Within the western calendar system it is impossible to tell when particular Muslim or traditional Balinese festivals will fall because the complex Balinese calendar system does not correspond to the western calendar. This is why the dates when festivals take place cannot be stated precisely.

In Java gamelan music is played at Muslim ceremonies, traditional festivities and shadow play performances...

Muslim festivals and ceremonies in Java

During **Ramadan** devout Muslims are not allowed to eat or drink from the time the sun rises to when it sets. But as soon as the sun has set, families and friends gather

together to eat the first meal after a whole day of fasting (Buka Puasa). In many regions, festivals and ceremonies take place just before Ramadan to celebrate the beginning of the month-long fast. These festivals are often celebrated in conjunction with markets where people can eat and drink to their heart's content before the long days of fasting start.

For instance in Kudus, in Central Java, people celebrate **Dandangan**, a street party that starts five days before the beginning of Ramadan. The centre of the city is completely taken over by stalls selling toys and food, and most people regale themselves with a dish typical of Kudus, namely *soto kudus*, a milky chicken soup. The atmosphere becomes increasingly festive and reaches a peak on the eve of Ramadan until drums announce the beginning of the month of fasting.

The most important Muslim festival in Indonesia, and indeed the rest of the world, is **Idul Fitri** or **Lebaran**, which marks the end of Ramadan. Throughout the archipelago it is marked by frantic travelling, resembling some kind of mass migration. People everywhere want to return to their families and their home towns or villages to celebrate this important festival, enlivened by fireworks and torchlight processions. Prayer meetings are organised everywhere in mosques and public spaces. Families get together to enjoy a festive meal, which is an important part of this ceremonial festival. In addition, many towns and villages organise special events to mark the occasion. For instance, in Wendit, near Malang in East Java, there is a festival that starts in the middle of Ramadan and continues throughout the last eleven days of the fast. The climax is on the eleventh day, when dancers jump into the local lake in the hope of achieving eternal youth. This illustrates how local Indonesian traditions have also become integrated into the Islamic religion.

The end of Ramadan is also celebrated with splendid festivities in Yogyakarta.

... and at performances of epics from the Ramayana.

The Grebeg Syawal ceremony starts at 8 o'clock in the morning in praise to Allah and gratitude to the Almighty. The ceremony concludes with a parade of the guards of the Kraton, the old sultan's palace, wearing the magnificent traditional uniform, walking towards northern Alun-Alun, the central square in front of the Kraton. At the end of Ramadan, orphans and widows are offered gifts and presents.

Indonesian Muslims also celebrate the "day of sacrifice", **Idul Ad'ha**, the day when Abraham tried to offer his son Isaac as a sacrifice to God. Mass prayer meetings take place in mosques and public places. Lambs are slaughtered and the meat is distributed to the needy.

The birthday of the Prophet Mohammed, **Maulid Nabi Muhammad**, is also an important festival in the Muslim calendar, providing yet another opportunity to organise ceremonial folk dances and processions. The main centres of attraction are the old sultan's palaces in Yogyarkarta and Solo (Surakarta) where lavish events attract crowds from all over Indonesia. The festivities include a magnificent procession, as lavish as that of Idul Fitri, from Kraton to the mosque. On arrival there, religious leaders bless the offerings and these are later distributed among the faithful. Placed on fields, the belief is that these offerings will ensure a plentiful harvest. This is also an opportunity to hear the famous gamelan orchestras of the sultan's palaces. Virtually a must on this day is *wajik*, a sweet brown rice dish whose colour and flavour is enhanced by brown palm sugar or cakes made with brightly coloured rice.

Non-Muslim festivals on Java

Although Java is dominated by Islam, preserved on the island is **Borobudur**, one of the largest and most important holy Buddhist centres in the world, a symbol of Buddhism and a testimony to its glorious past. This is the place where **Waisak**, the

birthday or rather the "Enlightenment" of Siddharta Gautama, the historic Buddha Shakyamuni, the Enlightened One of the House of Shakya, is celebrated every year on 22 May. On that day, an important procession of monks and pilgrims makes its way with holy water from the small temple of Mendut, an "outpost" of Borobudur, to Borobudur itself, the temple erected by the Shailendra dynasty in the 8th and 9th century.

But there are even older rituals in Java that are still celebrated by the inhabitants. For instance, the fishermen in Jepara (Central Java) and many other villages of the island are very loyal to their traditions. One such tradition is the festival of **Lomban**, whose central element is the ceremony of the water buffalo head, which the men of the village throw into the sea together with other offerings. This ceremony is all about fertility and prosperity; traditionally, Java as well as Bali has always been a male-dominated society. The religious rituals are completed by popular events including a boat race and a "fight between fishermen and pirates", evoking memories of a distant past.

In Banyuwangi in East Java, the Hindu festival of **Mekiyi**, takes place on the eve of Nyepi, the Balinese New Year. In Balinese Hinduism, evil is believed to come from

> "In Bali and also in Java, processions often lead to the sea. The evil that threatens from the deep must be pacified, the sea must be cleansed and purified."

A nourishing break on the edge of a crater in the Tengger region.

the sea: the sea is dirty and unclean and it harbours an evil Underworld. This is why the purification of the sea is an ever-recurring ritual. The ceremony begins at the temple of Pura Agung Tawang and ends near the sea, which is then presented with sacrificial offerings.

Rivers and places where rivers flow into each other are endowed with a special spiritual power in Balinese Hinduism. For instance, every year people celebrate **Rebo Wekasan**, a special water ceremony held at the confluence of the Opak and Gajah Wong rivers on the last Wednesday of the month of Sapar. Those present pray that the soil should remain fertile and the harvest plentiful. The festival lasts a whole week and ends in the Permuni caves where, according to legend, Panembahan Senopati met the goddess of the South Seas.

The Tengger tribe is a minority ethnic group of people who inhabit the mountainous volcanic region of Bromo. Completely cut off from modern life, they still live according to the customs and traditions of their ancestors, similar to those of the Bali Aga on Bali. Their ancestors remained here when the old aristocracy of the Majapahit kingdom escaped from the Muslim invasion in the 15th century to settle in Bali. Every year, on the 14th or 15th day of the month of Kesada (according to the Tengger calendar) the Tengger celebrate a special ceremony on the edge of the Bromo crater. It is based on the legend of Roro Auteng and Joko Seger, descendants of the Majapahit dynasty and legendary ancestors of the Tengger (Auteng and Seger = Tengger) of today.

The couple had remained childless for a long time. In despair, they promised the volcano god their youngest offspring if he would grant them children. The god of Bromo accepted their offer and granted their wish. However, the parents did not keep their side of the bargain. The volcano god therefore decided to help himself: he seized the 25th child and carried him into the crater. The child let it be known that he was happy to sacrifice himself so long as this led to harmony between the people and the mountain in the future.

In order to preserve this harmony, the Tengger commemorate and renew this ancient sacrifice with pacifying rituals and offerings. As the sun sets, the priests begin to prepare the offerings – rice, flowers and fruit – brought by the thousands of believers. Having blessed the offerings at the foot of the mountain, the priests then convey the wishes of the Tengger to the god of the volcano. Finally, the crowd of the faithful climb the mountain up to the edge of the crater where the offerings are thrown into the clouds of smoke rising from it. As a result the Betoro Bromo will bless and protect the people for another year.

The Balinese calendar

The Balinese calendar is extremely complicated. Not one but two calendars are used to calculate the date of religious festivals and other major events in the year. The Saka calendar which originates in India is based on the cycle of the months. A Saka year has 355 days, which are divided into months of 29 or 30 days. Every 30 months a bissextile or leap year month is necessary in order to synchronize the lunar and solar years. The Balinese calculate the day of Nyepi, the Balinese New Year, which falls in spring, on the basis of the Saka calendar. Many temple festivals are also calculated on the basis of this calendar according to the full moon, which is always considered the most favourable time.

The Pawukon or Wuku calendar is far more complex than the Saka calendar. To the outsider, this calendar consists of a confusing system of three-day, five-day, six-day, seven-day and ten-day weeks that are calculated in parallel, forming a cycle of 210 days. In addition, the Pawukon calendar is divided into 30 seven-day units, *uku*, and 35 six-day units, *tumpek*. However, the five-day and seven-day cycles are the most important.

The omen of each day varies according to which day of the seven-day week corresponds with which day of the five-day week. Specialists predict which are the most favourable days for temple festivals, weddings, cremations on the basis of the particular combination of the cycles of the days. They are helped in this by the Palelintangan: six rows of seven pictures are arranged in rows above one another, the divinities of the weekdays being represented by one of the horizontal seven-day rows. As far as the annual festivals are concerned that are calculated on the basis of this East Javanese-Balinese calendar it is possible that in certain circumstances they will occur several times within the western calendar because the Pawukon calendar has only 210 days.

Above left and page opposite: Gebogans, the beautiful, heavily decorated "tree offerings", are an indispensable part of every temple festival in Bali.
Above right: Cremation ceremonies for the departed are also magnificent occasions.

Festivals in Bali

There are several categories of rituals and festivals in Bali. Among the most popular ones – not only with Indonesians but also with tourists – are the Dewa Yadnya rituals, ceremonies in honour of Hindu-Balinese divinities, and the Sanghyang Widhi Wasa. This category of festivals also includes Odalan, rituals commemorating the foundation or consecration of a temple.

Because there are so many temples in Bali – there are over 10,000 temples on the island even without counting the house and family temples – visitors will have little difficulty in experiencing such a festival. There are temples whose anniversary is calculated on the basis of the Saka calendar; these are mostly ones that were founded before the 16th century. The anniversary of other temples is calculated on the basis of the Pawukon calendar. When the date of the festival is determined byf the Saka calendar, the date usually falls on a full moon, although in the case of a temple of the Underworld (Pura Dalem), the date will fall on a new moon. But if the Pawukon calendar has been used, the dating of festivals becomes much more complicated. According to the Pawukon calendar, the most favourable days are the Kajeng Kliwon days (when the last days of the three-day week coincide with the last day of the five-day week) or the period around Galungan or Kuningan. The calculation of the dates of festivals is a science in itself.

The complicated and extremely elaborate preparations for Odalan start several days before the festival . The offerings must be prepared: food is bought, bamboo plaited, and columns of offerings known as *gebogan* are constructed. On the day of the festival, women carry the columns of offerings, beautifully made from fruit, pastries, rice and other items to the temple to be blessed by the priest. Some *gebogan* are particularly magnificent: fruit, eggs and flowers are attached to the trunk of a banana tree. After being offered to the gods in the temple and blessed by the

Cockfighting is now forbidden except during temple festivals.

priest, the food is consumed at home within the family. Odalan are joyful festivities during which the Balinese are allowed to indulge in a former "national sport" that is otherwise forbidden: cockfighting. This gruesome pastime has a religious background, in that the blood shed by the cock is seen as an offering to the spirits of the Underworld. It is also an opportunity for performances of *wayang kulit* (shadow theatre) or episodes from the Ramayana, the Indian heroic epic. The most lavish celebration of Odalan takes place in the most important temple in Bali, the Pura Besakih or Mother temple.

The date of the Balinese New Year, **Nyepi**, is calculated on the basis of the Saka calendar and is celebrated around the day of the equinox in March. New Year's Eve is celebrated with offerings and ceremonies whose aim is to pacify the evil spirits. In the evening, children and young people take to the streets where they make as much noise as possible with gongs, cymbals and bangers – the noise must be loud to make the spirits disappear. New Year's Day itself is characterised by complete silence: should the spirits driven away from the island want to return, they must be made to believe that everyone on Bali is dead, so that they will go away again.

The festival of **Galungan and Kuningan** – that is the period between these two days – is typical of Balinese Hinduism. It is a festival calculated on the basis of the Pawukon cycle and is therefore celebrated every 210 days. During this period, the deified ancestors are present in the family temples, while the gods fight the demons and defeat them. The gods never destroy the evil spirits entirely. It is always a matter of balance: the balance between good and evil and the fact that that one cannot exist without the other.

Places of interest in Bali and Java

Bali

Bali is the island of beaches, rice fields and ancient Balinese Hindu temples. Anyone visitor to Bali is bound to encounter the sound of bamboo flutes, cymbals, stringed instruments, gongs and drums. The source of the music will probably be a temple ceremony, a gamelan orchestra, a procession carrying offerings to the sea or to the temple – or a body carried to the place where it will be cremated. Walking along the streets, visiting a boutique or wandering a hotel: offerings to the gods are everywhere to be seen, consisting of beautiful wickerwork made of bamboo or of palm leaves filled with rice or exotic flowers. This is because Bali is indeed the "island of the gods".

The inhabitants of Bali do not worship a single god but many different gods or divinities: the forces of good and evil, light and darkness, heaven and the underworld, mountains and the sea. It is these last two that form the central pairing in Balinese religious belief and around which the other pairings are arranged. The mountain is Kaja, divine and holy, bringer of fertility, and residence of gods and the spirits of ancestors and deified natural forces. Kelod, the sea, on the other hand, is home to demons and evil spirits, the forces of the underworld. In between is the earth where people live. Remembering this, the layout of Balinese farmsteads and villages immediately becomes understandable. Every village has at least three temples that are arranged on a (purely imaginary) axis from the mountain to the sea. The *pura*

The waters of Lake Batu are regarded as sacred.

puseh, the temple of origin, is dedicated to the deified ancestors, the founders of the village, and as such it stands on the Kaja side, nearest to the holy mountain. The *pura desa* stands in the centre of the village and acts both as village hall and temple. Finally the *pura dalem*, the temple of the underworld, dedicated to Durga, the goddess of death, stands on the Kelod or seaward side of the village, and is where people come to be in contact with the forces of the underworld.

But there are also a number of other centres of worship in the village in addition to these three temples. These centres of worship often reflect the various trades of the villagers. For instance, the fishermen have a temple for the gods of the sea and rice farmers have a temple dedicated to the rice gods where people present their offerings to the rice goddess. As well as these, there are family temples and shrines built in special places such as at the confluence of rivers, springs and the like. The number of temples in Bali is enormous.

Bangli: The three terraces of Pura Kehen, built on the side of the mountain, are situated just outside the small town of Bangli, a former royal city. The buildings date from the 11th century and are recognized as one of the most fascinating temple complexes on the island. Particularly impressive sights are the eleven-tiered *meru* (tapered shrine) with its remarkable carvings and woodwork, and the divine Hindu trinity of Brahma, Vishnu and Shiva on a lotus throne.

Batur, Lake: This large lake has formed in the crater of an old volcano, while the active volcano Mount Batur has formed in its centre. Its behaviour is unpredictable, yet villages have sprung up both on the edge of the crater and inside the caldera. One such village is Trunyan, inhabited by the Bali Aga who differ from their "cousins" in Tenganan in their funeral traditions: they wrap their dead in a white shroud and take them to a place outside the village where they leave them to decompose. The idea behind this practice is that wild animals will transport the remains of the departed to the hereafter.

Bedulu and Pejeng: Today Bedulu is a small village that has lost all its former glory and importance. Indeed, it used to be the centre of the kingdom of Pejeng. The name Pejeng is mainly associated with a unique archaeological find – the Moon of Pejeng, the largest known bronze drum dating from prehistory. But it is still a mystery where it comes from and who made it. It can be seen in the temple Pura Penataran Sasih.

Slightly south of Bedulu is another unsolved mystery: the enormous stone relief of Yeh Pulu, a unique masterpiece – indeed there is nothing like it in the rest of Bali or Java. The frieze depicts Ganesh, the elephant god, the "child" of Shivas and Parvati, and other secular subjects.

Besakih, Pura: This is the "Mother temple", the most important temple for all Hindus in Bali. Its history dates back to the 11th century. Every important

Pura Besakih is the most important Hindu temple complex in Bali.

> "Waters from the mountains are symbolic of fertility. Pura Ulun Danau Bratan is a temple dedicated to the goddess of lakes and rivers."

family and every village has a shrine here. The complex consists of three main temples and countless subsidiary temples. The largest temple is Pura Panataran Agung Besakih, dedicated to Sanghyang Widhi Wasa, the Most High, portrayed here in the shape of Shiva. To complete the Hindu Trinity, the Pura Besakih is flanked by the Pura Kiduling Kreteg dedicated to Brahma and the Pura Batu Madeg for Vishnu. The visitor should not be put off by the climb – the view from the top across the roofs of the surrounding temples and the landscape is absolutely spectacular.

Bratan, Lake: Like Lake Batur, Lake Bratan (together with two other lakes) is also situated in the crater of a volcano. Nevertheless the vegetation is green and luxuriant and the mountain is often shrouded in swathes of mist. It is not surprising therefore that the water of the lake is said to bring fertility to the fields. There is an idyllic temple, Pura Ulun Danau Bratan, built on two small islands off the west shore of Lake Bratan. It is dedicated to Dewi Danau, the goddess of lakes and rivers. The temple is adorned with an eleven-stepped *meru*, a tapering shrine dedicated to Shiva and Parvati.

Craftwork Streets: Along the road from Denpasar to Ubud are a series of famous centres grouping the best-known craft workshops in Bali, specialising in all the Balinese crafts: *batubulan* (stonemasonry craftwork), *celuk* (gold and silverware), *batuan* (paintings by young artists), *mas* (woodcarvings), and finally Ubud itself with its neighbouring villages, particularly known for their painting workshops.

Denpasar: The capital of the island tries very hard to match Jakarta, on the wholewithout much success. However, there are a some interesting places which are definitely worth visiting. The Museum Bali , on the south-east side of Puputan Square, is a museum of ethnology, built in the traditional

architectural style of a palace or temple. The exhibits includ Topeng masks, shadow theatre puppets, craftwork and paintings. There are also interesting models representing the major ceremonies in the life of a Balinese. On the north side of Puputan Square stands Pura Jagatnatha, one of the Balinese imperial temples, dedicated to the Most High, Sanghyamng Widi Wasa. The church of St Joseph is an interesting example of the fusion of styles and cultural traditions. This Catholic church, situated in Jalan Kepundung, is a perfect example of an architectural style that combines both Balinese and European elements. Those interested in Balinese art should pay a visit to the Werdhi Budaya Art Center in Jl Nusa Indah. It houses fascinating permanent exhibitions of paintings and wood carvings by Balinese artists. There is also a gallery with paintings by the German artist Walter Spies.

A spirit of the Underworld guards the entrance to the elephant grotto, which contains relics both of Buddhism and Hinduism (left). The Wayang paintings in Klungkung depict everyday scenes, various divinities, and stories from heroic epics.

Goa Gajah: The "elephant cave", a Hindu-Buddhist shrine, 4 km/½ miles south-east of Ubud, is definitely worth a visit.

Gunung Kawi: 13 km/8 miles north-east of Ubud are the so-called "royal tombs". These are memorials to deified kings and their spouses, with a height of about 7 m/23 ft.

Klungkung: Klungkung looks back on a proud history as capital of the Gelgel or Klungkung kingdom. Founded after the fall of the Majapahit dynasty at the end of the 15th century, the Klungkung kingdom and its rulers played a major role in the history of the island until 1908. At the beginning of the 20th century, the Dutch took action against all who resisted colonisation. This finally led to the *puputan*, a ritual mass suicide in front of the tower of the palace – which the Dutch then proceeded to destroy.

Only two of the ancient buildings have survived, Kerta Gosa and Bale Kembang, both situated in a small park (Taman Gili). The law courts and

> "The beautiful sea temple, Pura Tanah Lot, was built to keep at bay the demons of Underworld who lived in the sea."

"floating" royal pavilion are decorated with very interesting paintings in the so-called Wayang style.

Luhur Batukau, Pura: This mountain temple, situated on the south-eastern slope of the volcano Gunung Batukau, is dedicated to Mahadewa, the god of the volcano. It is one of the imperial temples much visited by pilgrims.

Mengwi: Mengwi used to be the centre of an ancient kingdom, and this little town still boasts one of the most beautiful temples in Bali, the Pura Taman Ayun. This splendid imperial temple, surrounded by a mass of lotuses, is laid out around three courts inhabited by the ancestors of the royal House of Mengwi. The temple dates back to 1637 but was enlarged in the 19th century.

Pejeng: See Bedulu and Pejeng

Sangsit: Sangsit, situated in the north of Bali, boasts two temples of particular interest. The Pura Beji is built in typical north-Balinese style with magnificent carvings of foliage, arabesques and demons. Characteristic of northern Balinese architecture is the unique main hall, in this case is dedicated to Dewi Sri, dominating the complex. While in Sangsit, the Pura Dalem Sangsit can also be visited. This is a temple dedicated to the underworld, decorated with crudely explicit reliefs.

Sanur: The village Sanur is frequently associated with the ethnologist Margaret Mead and the painter Le Mayeur. Originally an idyllic fisherman's village, it attracted many artists and intellectuals. Then came the tourists. Besides the attractions of sea and sand, the Le Mayeur museum is also worth a visit. Here you can admire paintings by the Belgian artist Jean Le Mayeur who lived in Sanur with his wife, Ni Pollok, a celebrated Legong dancer.

Tanah Lot, Pura: This temple, situated in a breathtaking location, is undoubtedly the most beautiful of all the sea temples. Erected on a rock jutting out to sea, it was built to keep at bay the demons of underworld who lived in the sea. The sight of Tanah Lot at sunset is absolutely breathtaking and quite unforgettable.

Tenganan: This fortified village is situated above Candi Dasa. It is still inhabited by the Bali Aga, the original Balinese inhabitants, who have preserved many of the pre-Hindu traditions. Life in Tenganan is regulated by a complex set of social rules and its inhabitants are determined to preserve their old customs and traditions while also appreciating tourism. The Bali Aga of Tenganan still practise two ancient crafts, the transcription of ancient Balinese texts on the leaves of the Lontar palm, and the textile art of *geringsing* or double-ikat weaving (both warp and woof are tie-died). Double-ikat wares are extremely rare (only faulty pieces are sold) because, as well as being time-consuming to make, they are thought to protect against illness and bad luck.

Tirta Empul, Pura: This important Hindu-Dharma shrine is situated about 15 km/9½ miles north-east of Ubud. It is erected near Indras, the spring of immortality. According to an inscription in ancient Balinese, this temple was founded in 962.

Terrifying figures guard the Temple of the Underworld on the outskirts of the city of Ubud.

Tirtagangga: Set in an impressive landscape of rice fields, these are the ruins of the Tirtagangga royal bathing pools, an ancient royal water palace.

Ubud with Peliatan, Campuan and Kedewatan: Ubud is only a small town but it is an important cultural centre and attracts artists from all over the world. This began in the 1930s when the artists' cooperative *Pita Maha* was founded by the artists Walter Spies and Rudolf Bonnet, supported by Cokorda Agung, a Balinese aristocrat, and in collaboration with I Gusti Nyoman Lempad, an important Indonesian artist. The aim was to encourage young Balinese artists and promote their work abroad. Ubud's streets are lines with countless galleries and souvenir shops. The Museum Puri Lukasan, set in magnificent gardens, houses modern Balinese paintings, wood carvings and sculpture.

The Agung Rai Museum of Art in Peliatan near Ubud is also worth a visit. It houses traditional and contemporary Balinese paintings as well as Javanese and foreign works of art.

Near the bridge to Campuan is a very unusual temple, the Pura Gunung Lebah. One of the oldest temples on the island, it stands in a very picturesque location, on the confluence of two arms of the Uos river and therefore a place of special spiritual power. It is dedicated to the rice goddess and also to the divinities of Lake Batur.

The Antonio Blanco Gallery in Campuan is the gallery-museum of the American artist Antonio Blanco who presents his surrealist work here.

The Neka Museum, in Kedewatan neat Ubud, specialises in 20th century

Rice terraces, typical of Bali.

Balinese painting and works by European artists who have lived in Bali for a long time.

Ulu Watu, Pura: Like Pura Tanah Lot, Ulu Watu is a sea shrine. It is situated in spectacular location on sheer cliffs.

Yeh Pulu: See Bedulu and Pejeng

Java

Java is large. Java is powerful. Java is the business, industrial and political heart of the Indonesia. It is largely but not entirely Muslim. But the island is also one of great contrasts. Not far from the powerful, all-devouring, consumer-dominated city of Jakarta, about two hours distant by car, there is a small enclave where time seems to have stood still, where the inhabitants have cut themselves off from the modern world and visitors are not welcome. In the Kendeng highlands in West Java, the Badui have preserved all their ancient traditions and reject anything that is artificial. They rely entirely on nature for their survival and depend on the spirits for protection and advice.

Chinese communities in the cities and towns have also preserved many of their ancient traditions, in spite of recurring problems with Indonesians.

Borobodur, the most important Buddhist temple complex in south-east Asia. Each of the small stupas conceals the figure of a Buddha.

The cities of Java are inhabited by people from all over the island who have long been attracted to the city by a desire to improve their situation. Naturally they brought their food with them, so the sweet cuisine of Central Java will often be found rubbing shoulders with the spicy Padang dishes from Sumatra, the Dutch-Indonesian rijstafel, Arab cuisine and Chinese dishes, influenced by the Nyonya culinary tradition.

Travelling around Java there are many wild and cultivated landscapes to be found: tea plantations in the west, fields on the Dieng plateau where potatoes and vegetables are grown, dry, arid crater landscapes alternating with green fertile countryside in the mountainous regions of East Java, and spectacular stretches of coastline such as the black beach of Parangtritis and the sheer cliffs of the east Javanese coast. Off the coast of West Java is Krakatoa, or rather the more recent volcano Anak Krakatau ("child of Krakatoa"), on the site of the catastrophic volcanic eruption in 1883, the largest ever recorded.

Bandung: This West Javanese university town is built in beautiful Dutch colonial style, reminiscent of Art Deco and very much worth a visit. The Geological Museum has the largest collection in south-east Asia, and it also contains the skull of "Java man" discovered near Sangiran. The Gedung Merdeka museum houses an exhibition about the Bandung conference held here in 1955.

Blitar: This relatively quiet little town is an ideal starting-point for expeditions. Candi Penataran is about 15 km/9½ miles away. This temple whose history dates back to the 12th century was once the most important place of worship in the Majapahit kingdom. It boasts beautiful reliefs depicting motifs from Indian epic poems. Not a beautiful building but very significant to

Hindu temple in the crater of the extinct Tengger volcano, at the foot of the Mount Bromo crater.

Indonesians is the tomb of Sukarno, the first president of the republic of Indonesia, which can be visited on the outskirts of Blitar.

Bogor: Bogor contains the palace of Buitenzorg ("Without a care"), built in 1745 and modelled on Blenheim Palace in England but later burnt down and rebuilt. The Botanical Gardens were laid out here in 1817 by the German Caspar Reinhardt and today they are much visited by people escaping from the hustle and bustle of Jakarta. Botanically it is still a unique natural treasure where the amazing range of Indonesian flora can be admired, from lotuses and lychees to rosewood trees.

Borobudur: Borobudur is the most important Buddhist temple complex in south-east Asia. It is situated some 40 km/25 miles from Yogyakarta. Erected in the 8th and 9th century under the Shailendra dynasty, it has been declared a world cultural heritage site. The giant step-pyramid consists of three main terraces, each representing one of the cosmic spheres of Mahayana Buddhism. It is best visited early in the morning when the light is not too strong and there are not too many tourists.

Bromo: It is worth coming early enough to watch the sun rise over Mount Bromo and Mount Semeru, the best viewpoint probably being Mount Penejakan. As the sun rises, plumes of smoke can be seen rising at regular intervals from Mount Semuru. Hissing and bubbling can be heard when crossing the caldera of the old Tengger volcano – in which the "new" volcano has developed – and climbing to the edge of the crater of Mount Bromo. This volcanic region is home to the Tenggerese, the only Hindu people in Java.

Candi Cangkuang: This temple is situated near Leles, some 20 km/12 miles north of Cipanas. Experts have not yet been able to date it accurately; it is between the 7th and 10th century, but whaterver the exact date, no other building of the Hindu-Javanese era is older than this temple, built on an island in a lake .

Candi Sukuh: This temple which is more reminiscent of a Mayan place of worship than of an Indonesian temple, is situated 30 km from Solo (Surakarta) on the western slope of Mount Lawu. Its date is uncertain and although a few inscriptions seem to point to 1416–59 it is possible that the temple could date from pre-Hindu times.

Cirebon: Once a sultan's town, Cirebon is now a major harbour town in northern Java and is also known as the town of crabs and *kerupuk* (*krupuk*). It is the largest production centre of *kerupuk*, the crab or shrimp crackers that are an indispensable part of every Indonesian meal. The palace of Cirebon, the Kraton Kasepuhan, is furnished in a colourful mixture of styles, combining Javanese as well as European and Chinese elements. The great mosque, the Masjid Agung, is magnificent example of Javanese architecture. Made entirely of wood, it was erected in the year 1500. Cirebon also has one of the oldest Chinese temples in Indonesia, the Thiaw Kak Sie. Just outside Cirebon is Taman Sari Sunya Ragi, the "pleasure palace" of a former ruler dating from about 1700.

Dieng Plateau: The journey to the Dieng Plateau is like travelling to another world. Leaving the world of rice fields and passing through fields planted with potatoes and vegetables, the route then goes through a volcanic landscape dotted with sulphur pools and thermal springs (there is a geo-thermic power station) to an ancient Hindu centre which used to be very important in the past. Candi Bima and the five shrines of the Arjuna group survivefrom what was originally a very much larger number (about 200), bearing witness to this glorious past.

Gedung Songo: A national park and nine Hindu temples make up Gedung Songo, a magnificent mountain landscape south of Semarang.

Gunung Kawi: Between Blitar and Malang, this holy place is popular with the Chinese, which is perhaps surprising since two members of the family of the Sultan of Sura or Yogyakarta have been buried here. People visit this place to pray for success and prosperity.

Jakarta: Jakarta originated with the former Dutch city of Batavia. But there is very little left of this colonial past, just a few traces on the road from Sunda Kelapa, the large port built for merchant sailing ships, running past the fish market (near the ruins of the ancient Dutch fort) to Kota, where the old Batavia was founded. The Chinese quarter is a fascinating place and worth a visit. Walking around this part of the city, evidence of the Chinese influence on Indonesian cuisine is omnipresent: mouthwatering smells emanate from the numerous eating places. Here there are delicious meat, fish and chicken dishes, flavoured with all kinds of spices while the distinctive aroma of Chinese medicinal herbs mixes with the delicate fragrance of joss sticks, burnt as offerings to the gods in the temple of Yinde Yuan.

Naturally, Jakarta also has many museums. The Wayang Museum in Fatahillah Square houses an interesting collection of *wayang kulit* (shadow puppets) while the Museum of Fine Arts, also in Fatahillah Square, specialises in contemporary Indonesian art and also has ceramics section with exhibits from the Majapahit period. The National Museum, another in the same square, has a treasure chamber (only open on Sundays) with valuable ceremonial objects in gold, often decorated with precious stones, such as the famous kris, the traditional Malay dagger or sword that spread throughout Indonesia. The collections also include objects from pre-history, early history and the Hindu-Javanese period as well as ethnographic exhibits. On Medan Merdeka is the History Museum, a national Indonesian monument. Those who are interested in the various types of houses in Indonesia should visit Taman MiniIndonesia, an open-air museum on the outskirts of town. It gives an excellent overall view of the various types of houses and building styles that can be found in the 27 Indonesian provinces.

Kudus: This city is famous for two reasons. First, it is one of the most important towns in the Muslim history of the country, and secondly, it is one of the largest production centres of kretek, the well-known Indonesian cigarettes flavoured with cloves. Kauman, the old part of the town, with its mid-16th century Al Menara mosque is definitely worth a visit. The kretek museum, situated in Getas, 3 km/2 miles outside Kudus, shows visitors how cigarettes are made.

Malang: Malang is a pleasant town with an agreeable climate. Even in colonial times, there were luxury country residences in the mountainous hinterland, in the hill resorts of Batu and Selecta. The Chinese temple En An Kiong in Jl Klenteng, the Chinese quarter of Malang, is of particular interest. Every one can worship here because the temple complex includes Buddhist, Daoist and Confucian shrines.

There are also some interesting Hindu or rather Hindu-Buddhist temples on the outskirts of Malang that are well worth a visit: Candi Kidal, Candi Jago, Candi Panataran and Candi Singosari, as well as the Buddhist Stupa Candi Sumberawan erected in 1351 on the site of a spring.

The Chinese in Indonesia have preserved their traditions. The temple of En An Kiong in Malang houses Buddhist, Daoist and Confucian shrines.

Pandaran: This once idyllic fishing village is increasingly becoming part of the tourist trail. However, a drive along the coast and a visit to the neighbouring villages are highly recommended. The stretch of road to Bojong Gebang is lined with a row of small family businesses that produce *tahu* (tofu or bean curd), tempe and *kerupuk*, making a n interesting visit for those who are interested in more traditional Indonesian food.

Parangtritis: Situated 27 km/17 miles south of Yogyakarta, this is where the sea goddess Loro Kidul is worshipped. Black, sandy beaches, sheer cliffs and a deceptively calm ocean are some of its attractions. Local people come here twice a week to bring offerings to Loro Kidul, while in Labuhan the cult of the goddess is associated with the sultans of Yogyakarta and Solo.

Prambanan: Situated 16 km/10 miles north-east of Yogya, this Hindu temple was erected in the mid-9th century by the Hindu Mataram dynasty as a counterpart to the Buddhist complex of Borobudur built by the Sailendra dynasty that they had driven out. Prambanan is vast, towering temple complex consisting of three areas. It also includes other smaller temples, both Hindu and Buddhist. On the edge of the temple complex is an open-air theatre where epic poems from the Ramayana are staged against the dramatic backdrop of the temple complex (not every day, often an abridged version).

Kerupuk drying on mats in Pangandaran.

The Hindu counterpart to Borobudur – Prambanan.

Semarang: One temple in this large bustling business city of over a million inhabitants is notable, the Sam Poo Kong. Both Chinese and Javanese come and worship in this temple, which was allegedly built by an envoy of the Chinese Imperial House in 1404.

Solo/Surakarta: Solo was once the capital of a sultanate. Two palaces have survived from the time of the sultanate, Kraton Kesunanan, built in 1745, and Puri Mangkunegaran, erected in 1866. The large reception hall of Puri Mangkunegaran is built in the manner of traditional wood constructions without any nails. The royal family still inhabits a side wing of the palace. Solo is also famous for its batik and visitors will be delighted with the wide range of these dyed textiles offer in Pasar Klewer.

Surabaya: The port of Surabaya is one of the largest industrial centres in the country after Jakarta. Tanjung Perak harbour is worth a visit to watch the Makassar schooners (ships built without nails) being loaded. Surabaya reflects the influence of other cultures and traditions on Indonesia. The narrow alleys Chinatown have elegant, tall houses and Chinese temples, while in the Arab quarter, Ampel Suchi, the narrow street that leads to the mosque, is like an oriental bazaar. In the European quarter there are still a few buildings to remind the visitor of the city's colonial past.

Trowulan: Near this village are a number of excavation sites and ruins of

In the Kraton, Yogyakarta.

temples dating from the time of the Majapahit kingdom (11th–14th century).

Yogyakarta: Yogyakarta is one of the old sultans' residences and capitals of Java. It has a fascinating historic centre built around the Kraton (palace) and the magnificent Taman Sari known as the "water castle", the former pleasure palace of the sultans. The quarters of batik craftsmen and antique dealers, south of Jl Prawirotaman and Jl Tirtopuran, are also fascinating. The main shopping street in Yogya is the well-known, busy Jl Malioboro, with the Pasar Beringharjo, a giant labyrinthine market of several floors where fruit, vegetables, meat and fish can bought as well as fabrics and every conceivable household item. In the evening the street turns into a giant snack-bar with stalls everywhere, selling mainly *gudeg* (chicken with jackfruit and coconut). Vsitors to the Kraton will find that it is divided into a northern and southern part, the latter being the more interesting. Every morning *wayang* (shadow play) performances are organised with wooden

puppets, naturally accompanied by a gamelan orchestra. A short distance away is Taman Sari, the former water gardens and bathing pools of the sultan, built in stone in 1761 but destroyed by an earthquake in 1867. Nevertheless, the old ruined walls are still fascinating. It is situated in an old quarter of the town with many small craft workshops, aimed at tourists, and the Pasar Ngasem (bird market) is nearby. Early in the morning (about 8 o'clock), visitors can admire many song birds and other magnificently colourful birds. There are also stalls selling vegetables, fish, spices and many other things.

To the north of the sultan's palace on Alun-alun is the Museum Sonobudoyo, which contains interesting objects from Java, Madura and Bali. The Museum Affandi includes works by the internationally famous Indonesian painter Affandi.

People who are interested in Javanese silversmithery should visit Kota Gede, 6 km/4 miles south of Yogya, known for its silver workshops where silver is still worked in the traditional manner.

Bird market and general market near Taman Sari.

Index of recipes

Alphabetical index of recipes

asparagus with crabmeat, Wild
    (Asparagus tumis kepiting) 99
aubergines (eggplants), Fiery
    (Terong bajak) 90
Avocado and coffee parfait
    (Es apokat moka) 119

bananas, Steamed cooking
    (Putu gedang) 120
beans, Sautéed asparagus
    (Cah kacang panjang) 85
beef sate, Balinese minced
    (Sate lilit sampi) 63
Beef with coriander seeds
    (Daging bumbu dèndèng) 56
Beef with red shallots and Chinese chives
    (Daging bawang) 57
Braised duck with banana flowers and
    pomegranate
    (Semur giring bèbèk) 50

cakes with black sticky rice and coconut
    cream, Small
    (Serabi hitam manis) 122
chicken à la Madame Berek, Fried
    (Ayam goreng Mbok Berek) 46
Chicken in coconut and curry sauce
    (Opor ayam) 49
Chicken in rujak sauce
    (Ayam bumbu rujak) 48
Chicken soup with traditional spices
    (Soto ayam) 36
Chicken stew with tomatoes
    (Semur ayam tomat) 45
chicken, Green (Ayam goreng ijo) 51
coconut cakes, Small (Kue Lumpur) 121

Crab with pineapple sambal
    (Kepiting kukus) 76
crabs in bamboo and coconut sauce, Small
    (Sambal goreng rebung yuyu) 75

Delicacies from the coconut islands
    (Rayuan pulau kelapa) 60
Duck à la Betutu (Bèbèk Betutu) 52
duck, Roast (Bèbèk panggang) 43

Fish in coconut cream sauce
    (Gulai bahari) 70
Fish or scampi in yellow bean sauce
    (Ikan/udang bumbu taoco) 71
fish soup, Sour-spicy (Karang asem) 40
fish with seaweed, Steamed
    (Ikan tim rumput laut) 82
Fruit and vegetable salad with palm sugar
    dressing (Rujak manis) 98

Lamb fillet with green pepper sauce
    (Kambing merica) 58
Lobster salad with coconut
    (Lobster dalam tempurung) 80
lotus root, Pickled (Acar teratai) 33

Meat and fish stew (Juanlo) 38
mussels, Fried (Tumis kerang) 82

Noodles with meat and mushroom ragout
    (Mie babah) 112
noodles with meat and vegetables, Fried
    (Mie jawa) 112
noodles with mixed vegetables, chicken
    and fish balls, Transparent
    (Telaga warna) 116

osso buco, Indonesian 64
oxtail soup, Spicy (Rawon) 39

oysters with red vinegar, Steamed
    (Tirem kukus cuka merah) 81

Pastry parcels cooked in stock
    (Pangsit kuah) 117
Pastry parcels stuffed with meat
    (Pangsit goreng) 117
pork chops, Glazed
    (Iga babi panggang) 55
Pork cutlets in date and mushroom sauce
    (Babi cin) 65
Poussin in pineapple and coconut sauce
    (Kleting kuning) 44

Quail bacang (Bacang burung dara) 43
Quails' eggs in coconut cream
    (Telur puyuh petis) 87

rabbit opor, Saddle of, with lily flowers
    and green tea leaves
    (Opor kelinci gigit daun) 67
Red snapper in red sauce
    (Ikan bumbu Bali) 72
relish, Yellow-coloured (Acar kuning) 32
Rice cooked in a clay pot (Nasi liwet) 101
Rice in a banana leaf
    (Lontong cap goh meh èbès) 108
Rice in coconut milk (Nasi uduk) 104
"Rice of fulfilment" (Nasi kabuli) 103
Rice with chicken in coconut milk
    (Nasi ayam santen) 104
rice, Fried (Nasi goreng) 106
rice, Steamed sticky (Ketan) 107
rice, Yellow (Nasi kuning) 102

Salad with peanut and potato dressing
    (Lotèk) 93
Sambal bajak 23
Sambal bawang putih 31

INDEX OF RECIPES | 151

Sambal cuka 29
Sambal goreng 24
Sambal jeruk 29
Sambal kecap 23
Sambal kecap brambang bawang 25
Sambal kelapa 31
Sambal kemangi 29
Sambal kemiri 31
Sambal manis 28
Sambal petis 26
Sambal sayur asin 26
Sambal taoco 24
Sambal teri 25
Sambal terong 25
Sambal trasi 29
Sambal ulek 23
sambal, Pineapple 26
sambal, tomato 28
sate, Aromatic (Sate wangi) 62
Scallops in jasmine tea (Mutiara) 81
Scampi with pandanus leaves
    (Udang pandan) 77
Scampi with pineapple (Udang nenas) 79
Sea bass in black sauce
    (Kakap goreng kecap) 74
Serundeng 34
Sesame balls stuffed with pineapple
    (Onde nenas) 119
soya bean (soybean) powder, Spicy-sweet
    (Koyah kedele) 35
Spring rolls (Lumpia basah) 114
Squid in kumquat sauce
    (Cumi cumi kenari) 83
sucking pig, Balinese (Babi guling) 66

tempe, Fried, or potato sticks
    (Kering kentang) 35
tofu (bean curd), and stuffed potatoes,
    Soup with (Sop tahu, kentang isi) 38
tofu (bean curd) and tempe, Spicy fried
    (Oseng oseng tahu tempe) 88
Tomatoes in sambal-goreng sauce
    (Sambal goreng tomat) 96
Tuna fish parcels with Savoy cabbage
    (Brèngkès tongkol, gubis) 71

Vegetable and coconut stew
    (Sayur lodèh waluh) 92
Vegetable balls (Gimbal mawut) 86
Vegetable curry (Sayur kare) 97
vegetable with coconut, Mixed
    (Urap urap) 87
vegetables with peanut sauce, Mixed
    (Gado gado Atim) 94
Wild boar in red rice wine
    (Cèlèng brem) 55

Yellow chicken curry with rice noodles
    (Laksa kemuning) 46

Recipes by category in order of appearance

Sambals, sauces and relishes
Sambal ulek 23
Sambal kecap 23
Sambal bajak 23
Sambal goreng 24
Sambal taoco 24
Sambal teri 25
Sambal terong 25
Sambal kecap brambang bawang 25
Pineapple sambal 26
Sambal petis 26
Sambal sayur asin 26
Tomato sambal 28
Sambal manis 28
Sambal trasi 29
Sambal kemangi 29
Sambal jeruk 29
Sambal cuka 29
Sambal kemiri 31
Sambal kelapa 31
Sambal bawang putih 31
Yellow-coloured relish
    (Acar kuning) 32
Pickled lotus root
    (Acar teratai) 33
Serundeng 34
Spicy-sweet soya bean (soybean) powder
    (Koyah kedele) 35
Fried tempe or potato sticks
    (Kering kentang) 35

Soups
Chicken soup with traditional spices
    (Soto ayam) 36
Soup with stuffed tofu (bean curd) and
    stuffed potatoes
    (Sop tahu, kentang isi) 38
Meat and fish stew (Juanlo) 38
Spicy oxtail soup (Rawon) 39
Sour-spicy fish soup (Karang asem) 40

Poultry dishes
Roast duck (Bèbèk panggang) 43
Quail bacang (Bacang burung dara) 43
Poussin in pineapple and coconut sauce
    (Kleting kuning) 44
Chicken stew with tomatoes
    (Semur ayam tomat) 45
Fried chicken à la Madame Berek
    (Ayam goreng Mbok Berek) 46
Yellow chicken curry with rice noodles
    (Laksa kemuning) 46
Chicken in ruiak sauce
    (Ayam bumbu rujak) 48
Chicken in coconut and curry sauce
    (Opor ayam) 49
Braised duck with banana flowers and
    pomegranate
    (Semur giring bèbèk) 50
"Green chicken" (Ayam goreng ijo) 51
Duck à la Betutu
    (Bèbèk Betutu) 52

Meat dishes and sate
Glazed pork chops
    (Iga babi panggang) 55
Wild boar in red rice wine
    (Cèlèng brem) 55
Beef with coriander seeds
    (Daging bumbu dèndèng) 56

Beef with red shallots and Chinese chives
(Daging bawang) 57
Lamb fillet with green pepper sauce
(Kambing merica) 58
Delicacies from the coconut islands
(Rayuan pulau kelapa) 60
Aromatic sate (Sate wangi) 62
Balinese minced beef sate
(Sate lilit sampi) 63
Indonesian osso buco 64
Pork cutlets in date and mushroom sauce
(Babi cin) 65
Balinese sucking pig (Babi guling) 66
Saddle of rabbit opor with lily flowers
and green tea leaves
(Opor kelinci gigit daun) 67

Fish and seafood

Fish in coconut cream sauce
(Gulai bahari) 70
Fish or scampi in yellow bean sauce
(Ikan/udang bumbu taoco) 71
Tuna fish parcels with Savoy cabbage
(Brèngkès tongkol, gubis) 71
Red snapper in red sauce
(Ikan bumbu Bali) 72
Sea bass in black sauce
(Kakap goreng kecap) 74
Small crabs in bamboo and coconut sauce
(Sambal goreng rebung yuyu) 75
Crab with pineapple sambal
(Kepiting kukus) 76
Scampi with pandanus leaves
(Udang pandan) 77
Scampi with pineapple (Udang nenas) 79
Lobster salad with coconut
(Lobster dalam tempurung) 80
Steamed oysters with red vinegar
(Tirem kukus cuka merah) 81
Scallops in jasmine tea (Mutiara) 81
Fried mussels (Tumis kerang) 82
Steamed fish with seaweed
(Ikan tim rumput laut) 82
Squid in kumquat sauce
(Cumi cumi kenari) 83

**Vegetable and tofu
(bean curd) dishes**

Sautéed asparagus beans
(Cah kacang panjang) 85
Vegetable balls
(Gimbal mawut) 86
Mixed vegetable with coconut
(Urap urap) 87
Quails' eggs in coconut cream
(Telur puyuh petis) 87
Spicy fried tofu (bean curd) and tempe
(Oseng oseng tahu tempe) 88
Fiery aubergines (eggplants)
(Terong bajak) 90
Vegetable and coconut stew
(Sayur lodèh waluh) 92
Salad with peanut and potato dressing
(Lotèk) 93
Mixed vegetables with peanut sauce
(Gado gado Atim) 94
Tomatoes in sambal-goreng sauce
(Sambal goreng tomat) 96
Vegetable curry (Sayur kare) 97
Fruit and vegetable salad with palm sugar
dressing (Rujak manis) 98
Wild asparagus with crabmeat
(Asparagus tumis kepiting) 99

Rice dishes

Rice cooked in a clay pot (Nasi liwet) 101
Yellow rice (Nasi kuning) 102
"Rice of fulfilment" (Nasi kabuli) 103
Rice in coconut milk (Nasi uduk) 104
Rice with chicken in coconut milk
(Nasi ayam santen) 104
Fried rice (Nasi goreng) 106
Steamed sticky rice (Ketan) 107
Rice in a banana leaf
(Lontong cap goh meh èbès) 108

Noodle dishes

Fried noodles with meat and vegetables
(Mie jawa) 112
Noodles with meat and mushroom ragout
(Mie babah) 112

Spring rolls (Lumpia basah) 114
Transparent noodles with mixed
vegetables, chicken and fish balls
(Telaga warna) 116
Pastry parcels stuffed with meat
(Pangsit goreng) 117
Pastry parcels cooked in stock
(Pangsit kuah) 117

Desserts and puddings

Sesame balls stuffed with pineapple
(Onde nenas) 119
Avocado and coffee parfait
(Es apokat moka) 119
Steamed cooking bananas
(Putu gedang) 120
Small coconut cakes (Kue Lumpur) 121
Small cakes with black sticky rice and
coconut cream
(Serabi hitam manis) 122

All the recipes and instructions given in this book have been carefully checked for accuracy. However, in the context of product liability or other legislation, the possibility of the existence of mistakes cannot entirely be excluded. Accordingly the recipes and instructions are provided without any guarantee by the authors or publisher. In particular, the authors and publishers accept no liability for any loss, damage or injury which may occur directly or indirectly as a result of following the recipes and instructions given or from individual behaviour or from failure to observe appropriate precautionary measures and safety guidelines.